Comida
CUBANA

A Cuban Culinary Journey

Brimming with creative inspiration, how-to projects, and useful information to enrich your everyday life, Quarto Knows is a favorite destination for those pursuing their interests and passions. Visit our site and dig deeper with our books into your area of interest: Quarto Creates, Quarto Cooks, Quarto Homes, Quarto Lives, Quarto Drives, Quarto Explores, Quarto Gifts, or Quarto Kids.

BURGESS LEA PRESS
donates 100 percent
of our after-tax profits
to food-related causes.

© 2017 Quarto Publishing Group USA Inc.
Text © 2017 Marcella Kriebel

First published in 2017 by Burgess Lea, an imprint of The Quarto Group Inc.,
401 Second Avenue North, Suite 310, Minneapolis, MN 55401 USA. Telephone: (612) 344-8100 Fax: (612) 344-8692

QuartoKnows.com

Burgess Lea titles are also available at discounts in bulk quantity for industrial or sales-promotional use. For details contact the Special Sales Manager by email at specialsales@quarto.com or by mail at 401 Second Avenue North, Suite 310, Minneapolis, MN 55401 USA.

10 9 8 7 6 5 4 3 2 1

ISBN: 978-0-9972113-3-7

Library of Congress Control Number: 2017939411

Editors: Janer Bukovinsky Teacher, Kate Winslow, and Thom O'Hearn
Project Managers: Madeleine Vasaly and Alyssa Lochner
Art Director: Laura Drew
Layout: Danielle Smith-Boldt

Printed in China

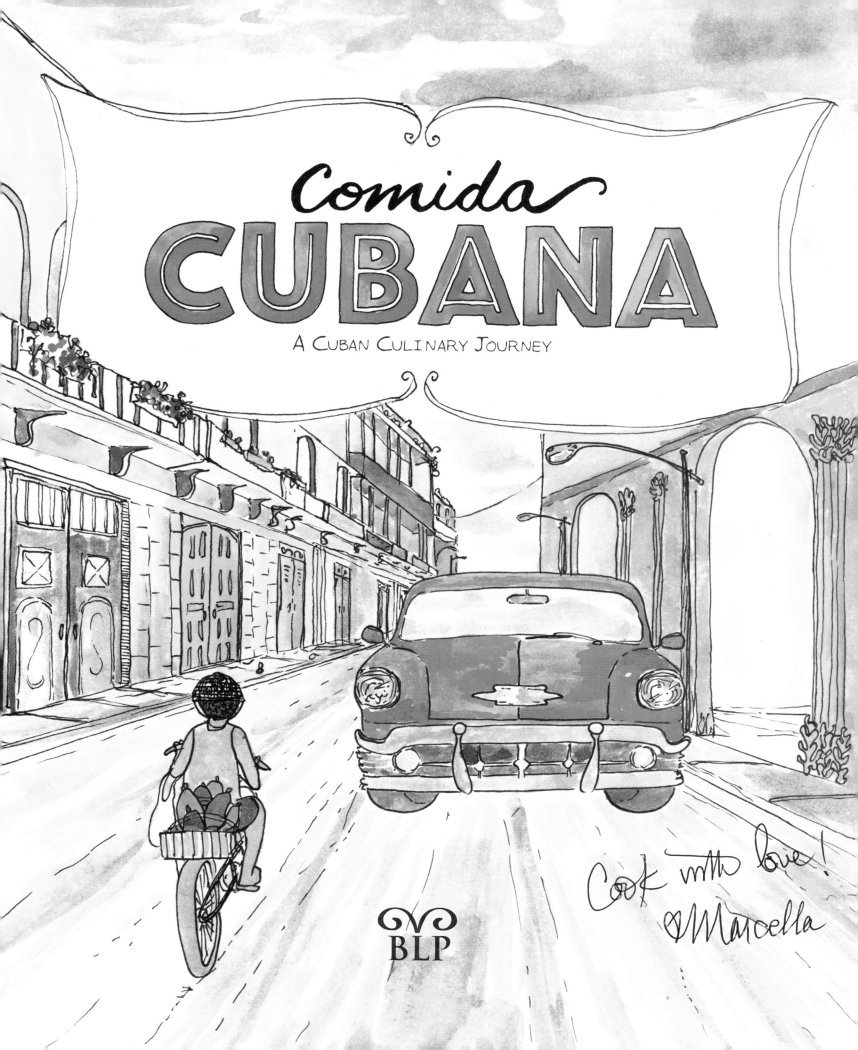

Table of Contents

Comida Cubana

A Cuban Culinary Journey

One afternoon, I opened the door to my little Havana apartment to find Pedro Duperey, a new friend I had met the week before, clutching a well-worn wooden mallet and a bag full of pineapples, malanga (similar to taro root), and mint. Pollo con piña (pineapple chicken) and mojitos were on the menu that afternoon, and he had come prepared for our day of cooking. As Pedro shuffled about the kitchen, he almost never let his mallet leave his side: He used it to crush ice, muddle mint, mash garlic cloves, hit a knife's blade through bone, and tenderize meat. The weathered wooden implement, perfectly contoured to Pedro's hand from years of use, came to symbolize what is so special about my experience cooking in Cuba. It's not the ingredients that set Cuban food apart, but rather the level of ingenuity, graciousness, and dedication to the craft of the people who prepare it. For me, this is what defines the charm of Cuban cooking.

I'm a visual artist by training, and in 2012 I wrote, illustrated, and self-published a cookbook of recipes that I picked up during my many travels throughout Latin America. Based on the success of Mi Comida Latina, I was offered the opportunity to create another book, this time focusing on the food and culture of Cuba. I had, however, never set foot on the island—a country that I only knew for its incredible music and mojitos. I had so much to learn. Excited, I approached this new book as I did my last one, with a genuine curiosity to learn about the people and their lives. I gathered recipes and narratives through a variety of cooking experiences lasting one year, recording them in a large journal as sketches and notes in both English and Spanish. I then fine-tuned each dish in my own kitchen, creating illustrated recipes inspired by my firsthand experiences.

I started my research close to home, in Philadelphia, where Maria Gonzalez shared dozens of dishes from her Cuban-American family with me. Her good friend, Emelio, often joined us, and over our multi-course meals, he recounted tales of his childhood in Cuba and memories of his mother in the kitchen. Emilio's stories brought to life the Cuban food culture I was learning so much about, lending context to classics and everyday staples such as harina de maíz (cooked cornmeal) and escabeche (fish marinated in vinegar). I smile when I recall his descriptions of parties where impressive stacks of bocaditos (little sandwiches) towered over his seven-year-old self, and the way his mother kept a loaf of pan Cubano (Cuban bread) in an elegant handbag hung near the door of their house.

I made my first trip to Cuba in March 2016, joining a small weeklong tour group to Havana organized by Veterans for Peace. This tour complied with the US State Department rules that permitted Americans to travel to Cuba legally as long as the purpose of the trip fit into one of twelve US government—approved categories, including "in support of the Cuban people" and "educational activities". Our itinerary, which included many typical tourist destinations, was a great introduction to the country, a fun cultural overview, and an informative experience. After my fellow travelers returned home, I stayed on in a small apartment in central Havana. There, I spent the next month connecting with locals willing to share their everyday dishes and stories of life on the island. I cooked with a variety of gracious locals, from my immediate neighbors to the plumber who came to fix my leaky sink. Sometimes we'd cook in their homes, but often we'd end up in my own little rented kitchen, after shopping for ingredients together. On any given day, I might have a specific dish that I wanted to learn, but my new friends were often eager to share one of their own favorites or a particular family recipe, and these dishes usually ended up being much more interesting. We would typically make several recipes together, sharing prep duties, while I asked questions and jotted down my notes in Spanglish, accompanied by little drawings of techniques in the margins. Then we'd sit down to enjoy our feast, often inviting neighbors or family members to join.

It was sheer luck that my first trip overlapped with the historic visits of Barack Obama, the first US President to visit Cuba since 1929, and The Rolling Stones, who performed the first major rock concert in the country's history. These two events reflected the excitement and potential for change felt by most everyone I met. "¡Por fin!" ("Finally!") people said. "¡Esto es sólo el comienzo!" ("This is only the beginning!") Others explained, "Cambios son despacio, pero sí, las cosas van a mejorar." ("Changes are slow, but yes, things are going to improve.") Cubans anxiously await a time when the US fully reinstates diplomatic relations and ends El Bloqueo, the embargo preventing trade between the two countries.

A few months later, I returned to Cuba to visit the eastern part of the island. The east has its own distinct type of cuisine, marked by dishes incorporating coconut milk, chocolate, and a singular approach to herbs and spices. In addition to learning from local home cooks, I learned recipes from several professional chefs in Holguín, Baracoa, and Santiago de Cuba. This trip expanded my view of Cuban cuisine immensely. I came to see a great breadth of flavors and dishes on the island beyond the classic lechón asado (roast pork) and arroz con pollo (chicken and rice). Recipes such as bacán, a mash of plantains and crabmeat steamed in a palm leaf, and natilla de chocolate, a chocolate pudding served in a cacao pod, lingered in my memory long after my visit. Shortly before I finished this book, Hurricane Matthew tore through the town of Baracoa, and it was painful to see images of destruction of the little town I came to love. During my trip, I had been heartened by the locals' incredible warmth and pride and inspired by their sense of ingenuity in their kitchens, many of which were in such humble settings. But one thing I know for certain—the people of Baracoa will say, "Hay que resolver." ("One must resolve the situation, and keep going"; see page 13.) True to what I've learned about the Cuban people, as much as they are exuberant towards everyday life, they are equally resilient in the face of hardship.

On Using This Book

I've spent the time since my visits to Cuba refining recipes, searching out the more unique ingredients called for, and turning my Washington, DC, apartment into a test kitchen. Many feasts later, I've paired the recipes with my illustrations, which began as pen-and-ink drawings and came to life with watercolor. To offer a deeper understanding of this unique island, I've added street scenes, landscapes, and narratives from my travels.

In this book, I've shared many classic, time-honored Cuban recipes, some simple and others more complex. As a person who loves big salads and eats a limited amount of meat, I had to acclimate to the customs of a Cuban diet because, generally speaking, classic Cuban food is heavy on starches and meat. While there was very little meat available during the *Período Especial* (the Special Period, page 77), by no means did that scarcity lessen Cubans' appetite for pork or beef. While I've included Cuban classics such as *Picadillo* (page 38) and *Vaca Frita* (page 37), I've also shared variations that reflect my own preferences. A meat broth, for example, can always be switched out for a vegetable broth. In addition, I've included many dishes that feature vegetables prominently, such as *Calalú* (page 89) and *Frituras de Calabaza* (page 113). Note: Many of the meat recipes involve large cuts of beef or pork that call for long marinating; it's a good idea to begin planning a day or two before.

I've done my best to share tips that make the preparation more efficient. Cuban kitchens are simple, devoid of most gadgets we take for granted. Ironically, Cuban cooks' most ubiquitous timesaving tool, the pressure cooker, is not one we are accustomed to using on a daily basis in the US (I include stovetop alternatives for such recipes). For grating and mixing ingredients, I often suggest using a food processor, even though this appliance is not readily available in Cuba. Most people do have a blender in their kitchens and use it regularly.

Cuba is an island steeped in many traditions, and is home to some of the kindest, most creative, and generous people I've ever met. I hope this book feeds your appetite and inspires your creativity for a Cuban adventure in your own kitchen!

Culinary Revolution, the Future of Food

Food evolves, as culture does; and we are just seeing the glimmers of a new era in Cuban cuisine. Though *Nuevo Cubano* has come of age in Miami, the island itself has yet to experience a major shift from the classic *Criollo* style (page 12). But the *Revolución Culinaria* is surely imminent.

A strong indicator of this culinary change is the increasing presence of privately owned and operated restaurants known as *paladares*. These independent establishments have existed legally since 1995, beside the long-standing nationalized restaurants. Initially, *paladares* had to serve food purchased at state-run stores or private farms (beef and lobster were prohibited), employ at least two family members, and could serve no more than twelve patrons. In 2011, nationwide economic reforms lifted many regulations, and *paladares* now outnumber state-owned restaurants and offer the most creative dishes on the island.

The sharp increase in tourism has brought major growth in the private restaurant offerings and a new motivation to create inspired cuisine. The island's tropical climate offers a wealth of fruits and vegetables and an established organic farming practice, providing high-quality produce. Greater access to outside resources coupled with improved cultural exchange should stimulate Cuba's food scene in exciting new directions.

Gaining Context

I'm including a timeline, perhaps unusual for a cookbook. I feel strongly about providing this framework as a reminder that history and politics directly impact food culture. This background and context helped me to understand the way average Cubans approach their food choices, availability of certain ingredients, and methods of preparation. Anthony Rossodivito, a friend and scholar of Cuban history, taught me so much about the island before my first visit. He helped me put together a historical timeline, and I've woven in some food-related facts as well (page 10).

As Anthony explained, in 1940, Cuban historian Fernando Ortíz likened the island and its culture to an *ajiaco*, a creole stew that combines elements from African, Spanish, and indigenous foods. Cuba truly is an *ajiaco*, part African and Spanish, distinctly Caribbean, with a resilient ingenuity that is uniquely Cuban.

I encourage people to dive deeper into Cuba's history to understand more about the dynamic and dramatic past of this little island. There is plenty that I am still trying to understand, like why most of Cuba's chicken comes from the American South despite the embargo, how okra became a common crop on the island, and why most people don't care for hot peppers. Cuba is like an onion; there are layers that lead to greater truths and evolving realities.

Anthony reminded me that in October of 1492, upon arriving on the island that would eventually become Cuba, Christopher Columbus declared it "the most beautiful and majestic land he had ever laid eyes upon." Through all its trials and tribulations Cuba is still beautiful, even in its constant state of cultural and political motion.

• 1901 Cuba Libre cocktail is invented

• 1899–1903 US military occupation of Cuba; Platt Amendment signed as precondition for the adoption of Cuban constitution (first of multiple interventions); US long-term lease of Guantanamo Bay begins

• 1917 US troops train for World War I on Cuban soil; Cuba produces record sugar harvest

1500s

• 1933 Fulgencio Batista leads the Sergeant's Revolt, Government of 100 Days begins

• 1934 Batista seizes power in military coup

• 1940 Batista elected president; 1940 constitution is written

1800s
• 1947 Eduardo Chibás forms Orthodoxo Party & battles corruption

• 1100–1450 Migration of Arawak, Taínos & Caribs to the island

• 1492 Columbus lands on the island of Cuba

• 1515 Santiago de Cuba founded by the Spanish

• 1520 First large group of 300 African slaves brought to work in the gold mines

• 1607 Capital moves to Havana

• 1795 Driven out of Haiti by the slave revolution, French colonists come to Cuba & develop coffee production

• 1951 Nitza Villapol's cooking show *Cocina al Minuto* begins 46-year run

• 1952 Batista seized power in military coup

• July 26, 1953 Fidel Castro leads attack on Moncada Barracks

• 1955 General amnesty for political prisoners; Fidel Castro leaves for Mexico to train guerrilla army & meets Che Guevara

• Nov 1956 The yacht Granma transports 81 revolutionaries & Fidel Castro to Cuba, guerrilla war begins in the Sierra Maestra known as the 26 of July Movement

1950s

• 1834 Construction of railway system begins to move sugar to ports

• 1847 First Chinese arrived in Cuba as contract laborers to work the sugar fields alongside Africans

• 1862 Bacardí, Boutellier & Company is formed, producers of some the most refined rum on the market

• Oct 10, 1868 Carlos Manuel de Cespedes begins Cuba's first war for independence (the 10 Years War), freeing his slaves & enlisting them to fight for independence from Spain

• 1887 Cuba ends its slave trade; more than 1 million African slaves were brought to Cuba primarily to work in sugar production

• 1892 Jose Martí founds the Cuban Revolutionary Party

• Feb 24, 1895 *El Grito de Baire*: the second war for Cuban independence begins

• July 1898 US intervention in Cuba, conclusion of the Spanish-Cuban-American War

 26 JULIO

1960s

• 1957–1958 Armed struggle in the cities & country against Batista (primarily student led)

• Dec 28, 1957–Jan 1, 1958 Che's column captures Santa Clara

• Jan 1, 1959 The Revolution comes to power

• May 17, 1959 Agrarian Reform Law signed: redistributes land to peasants, cooperatives & the state

• 1960 Cuba reestablishes relations with USSR & nationalizes major US industries; US stops importing Cuban sugar

• Jan 3, 1961 US breaks diplomatic relations with Cuba

• April 16–19, 1961 Bay of Pigs invasion; Fidel Castro declares socialist character of the revolution

• 1961 Literacy campaign established, raising literacy rate to 96 percent (it has been higher than this ever since)

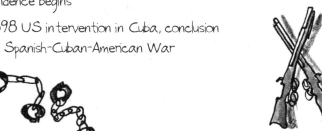

EVENTOS en la HISTORIA

- 1962 Ration system instituted in Cuba, a minimum amount of food & home basics available to all Cubans, items vary based on health & age, & tracked in a *libreta* (notebook)
- 1962 October Missile Crisis
- 1963 Che Guevara founds chocolate factory in Baracoa during his time as minister of industries

1970s

- 1963 USSR becomes Cuba's main trade partner
- 1966 First Coppelia ice cream parlor opens in Havana
- 1970 10 Million-Ton Sugar Harvest
- 1972 Government distributes thousands of stoves, pressure cookers & refrigerators
- 1975 Operation Carlota: Cuba sends volunteers to defend Angola's independence
- 1976 Socialist constitution written
- Oct 6, 1976 Cuban flight 455 bombed by Miami-based terrorists
- 1976 Cuba outlines renewed plan to grow tourism
- 1980 Mariel boatlift: more than 125,000 Cubans, many released convicts, flee to US

- 1980 Cuban farmers are granted permission to sell remaining produce above state quotas in unregulated markets
- 1985 A new housing law allows Cubans to purchase & sell property they rent from the government
- 1986 Food rationing is reduced & accounts for about 25 percent of individual consumption

1980s

- 1991–99 Special Period after the collapse of USSR
- 1992–93 Cuba's gross national product drops by more than ⅓ & exports are reduced nearly 80 percent
- 1995 Cuban authorities permit the first legal *paladares*, privately run restaurants, to operate (278 count)
- 2004 Honey production is an estimated 7,200 tons, the highest in the Caribbean

1990s

- 2008 Fidel Castro steps down, transfers presidential duties to younger brother, Raúl Castro
- 2008 Bans on private ownership of mobile phones & computers lifted
- 2015 US & Cuba begin dialogue to reopen relations
- 2016 Cuba & US open embassies for the first time since 1961, Fidel Castro dies at age 90

2000s

Comida Criolla & Cuban Cuisine

The term *comida criolla* refers to the cuisine of several Latin American countries where the traditions of the Spanish colonists blended with the flavors, crops, and cooking techniques of the indigenous people and the Africans brought there as slaves. Cuban food certainly embodies this tradition, and its Spanish and African influences are further flavored by French, Chinese, and American customs, all coming together to make the delicious stew that is Cuban cuisine today.

The strongest influences in Cuban cuisine come from the Spanish settlers, who arrived on the island in the late 15th century, and the Yoruba people of Africa, who were subsequently brought over as slaves after the Spanish had nearly extinguished the native population. With the Spanish came rice, beef, and pork, while Africans introduced okra, malanga, and plantains. These imports melded with several foods native to the island, including corn, yuca, peanuts, and squash; and today it's hard to imagine Cuban dishes without such variety.

Colonialism brought rapid change in the cuisine and flavors of the island. For instance, the hot, spicy chiles once cultivated and consumed by native populations, including the Taínos, Ciboneyes, and Guanahatabeyes, were essentially phased out of cultivation and replaced by the bell pepper and the *ají cachucha* (which looks like a habanero, but has a fruity flavor and lacks the heat) preferred by the Spanish. The presence of Louisiana-style hot sauces in Cuba is a holdover from centuries of trade between New Orleans and Havana. Rice cultivated in the American South was traded for Cuban sugar, and ports in those two cities flourished. Naturally, cultural and culinary influences were exchanged as well, including the picante sauce favored by the Haitian planter class who fled to both Cuba and New Orleans after the slave revolt in the late 18th century.

The influx of French Haitians at this time was very significant to the culinary landscape of the island. They introduced the *pastelitos* (pastries), which are a definitive part of the Cuban café tradition today. Light, fluffy turnovers filled with *picadillo* or guava paste are the favorite small bites of many Cubans at any hour of the day or night. The French are also responsible for the introduction of the coffee culture (page 107) and development of the coffee trade. Like the sugarcane industry, coffee production relied heavily on slavery, which remained legal until 1886 and in turn, impacted the demographics of the island.

The abolition of slavery by the United States and several European countries sparked a need to search for workers elsewhere, which instigated the first wave of Chinese immigrants, mostly men, who were promised work by the Cuban-Spanish planter class but at meager pay. As sugar production steadily increased, the first railroad was built in Latin America, entirely for the purpose of transporting sugar to the ports. Railroad construction brought the second wave of Chinese to Cuba, who arrived via San Francisco and New Orleans.

Although many Chinese left during and after the wars of independence from Spain (1868 and 1895), Havana grew to have the largest *Barrio Chino* (Chinatown) in all of Latin America during the mid-19th century and into the 20th century. A middle class of Chinese business owners developed, which included many Chinese restaurants. Although the Chinese population is relatively small, it has made a significant impact on Cuban cuisine. *Arroz frito* (fried rice), a popular dish found in Chinese restaurants, is often prepared at home, and *salsa china* (soy sauce) is a familiar condiment in the Cuban pantry.

Resolver: There's Always a Way & Cuban Kitchen Hacks

Resolver has come to occupy a very important place in the lives of Cubans in all areas of daily life. The Spanish word translates "to resolve," and it describes the very Cuban practice of "getting by" or "making it work," from keeping 1950s cars on the road to substituting powdered milk for fresh in a recipe. Every day, average folks prove that "necessity is the mother of invention." The ability to reinvent, repurpose, repair, and conserve when resources are limited or unavailable is a source of pride for Cubans. They have a strong sense of ingenuity and a drive to create solutions to meet their needs with whatever resources are at hand.

Throughout their history—from the War of Independence with Spain in the late 19th century to decades of suffering under the US trade embargo to the economic depression following the Soviet Union's breakup—Cubans have risen to the challenge of providing for themselves. The impact of the Soviet Union's demise on Cubans' daily lives cannot be overstated. Since the 1960s, Cuba had become very dependent on the USSR for all kinds of goods, especially food products. At least half of their daily caloric intake came from imports. Cuba found itself in dire straits due to the lack of support and trade with its main partner. During this time, known as *Período Especial* (the Special Period), Cuba had to move beyond producing mainly sugarcane to quickly converting their agriculture to crops to feed themselves. The country was able to pioneer intensive organic farming methods and implemented common-sense solutions for giving people access to food. For example, a system of small farms surrounding the urban areas eliminated the need to transport produce great distances, since petroleum was in short supply. In many cases, the concept of *resolver* became a matter of life and death. It was essential to follow the adage: "Use it up, wear it out, make it do, or do without."

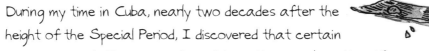

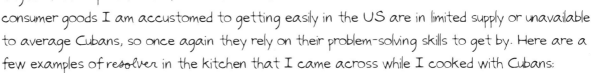

During my time in Cuba, nearly two decades after the height of the Special Period, I discovered that certain consumer goods I am accustomed to getting easily in the US are in limited supply or unavailable to average Cubans, so once again they rely on their problem-solving skills to get by. Here are a few examples of *resolver* in the kitchen that I came across while I cooked with Cubans:

- No ice cube tray? You can just freeze some water in the bottom of a plastic bowl and break it after.
- Need a nonstick surface for candies to set and don't have wax paper? Use wet newspaper.
- Need soup stock? Use the leftover water from cooking beans—nutritious and flavorful.
- No mortar and pestle? Mash garlic cloves with a rock on a cutting board.
- Don't have a sifter? Use a colander to sift dry ingredients.
- Need a salad dressing dispenser? Poke a hole in the cap of an empty plastic water bottle.

Baking pans & lunch trays repurposed to make an antenna.

Sazón Sofrito y Especias

Seasonings, Sauces, Marinades & Spices

For a dish to be truly sabroso (delicious), one must have a great sazón—that perfect mix of ingredients added to the dish, just the right way. It's safe to say that Cuban food is hearty and flavorful, but more subtle than one might imagine.

When it comes to flavor, it's the sofrito that acts as a foundation: Cubans consider the combination of fresh bell peppers (red or green), onion, and garlic to be the holy trinity of their cuisine. These 3 essential ingredients are sautéed with a bit of oil until soft. From there, additions may be made, including tomatoes and culantro (see glossary). Dry ground spices may be added later. This foundation forms the basis of most Cuban stovetop dishes: potajes (stews), frijoles (beans), and sopas (soups).

Cubans like spices, but use them carefully. Traditional Cuban food is much less picante (hot, spicy) than Mexican food, for example. When adding ground dried spices and discussing quantities, I learned so many phrases for "just a little bit." In measuring spices, this little bit was referred to alternately as la punta de la cuchara (the tip of the spoon), una media cucharadita (the half of a little spoon), un punto (a point, dash), or una pica/pisca (a point/a bit). Hot peppers are not often used in the dishes themselves. Instead, you'll often find a little bottle of hot sauce at the table. Although several types of mild peppers, such as the bell peppers and ají cachucha, are used often, the only hot pepper I encountered was the chile guaguao, a tiny pepper cultivated in the eastern part of Cuba, which generally has a more Caribbean influence.

Throughout the island, people grow their own herbs and spices. Many Cuban cooks who shared their kitchens with me had small potted gardens they tended on rooftops and balconies. Under the clotheslines, a variety of herbs could be found: oregano, chives, thyme, parsley, and mint were common. These fresh herbs were a source of both pride and thriftiness.

Lots of Cuban recipes call for sauces that can be made ahead and kept on hand for use in a variety of dishes. Mojo sauce is omnipresent in Cuba, and everyone has their preferred way of making it, depending on whether they use it to marinate fish or pork, or as a dressing for vegetables or salad. The word mojo, derived from the African Yoruba tradition, means "little spell" or "magic."

Mojo Clásico

Great on pork, yuca, or grilled fish, this recipe showcases naranja agria, sour orange (page 100). You can come close to achieving its flavor by mixing equal amounts of freshly squeezed orange juice with lime juice.

Makes about 1 cup (240 ml)

- ⅓ cup (80 ml) olive oil
- 6–8 garlic cloves, minced
- ½ cup (120 ml) sour orange juice
- ½ tsp ground cumin
- Salt and pepper to taste

Heat the olive oil in a pan over medium heat. Add the garlic and cook until lightly toasted, just 30 seconds. Don't let it brown or it will be acrid tasting. Add the sour orange juice, cumin, salt, and pepper. STAND BACK— the sauce may sputter! Add salt if needed; cool.

Mojo de Emelio

Emelio Companioni recounted how his mother would sometimes make this mojo with just the leftover cilantro stems, which lend the same flavor as the leaves. He stores this mojo sauce in the refrigerator and uses it throughout the week.

Makes about 1 cup (240 ml)

- ½ cup (25 g) cilantro stems, chopped
- ½ cup (120 ml) white vinegar
- ½ cup (120 ml) olive oil
- 3 garlic cloves, mashed
- Salt and pepper to taste

Combine all ingredients in a jar and shake well to blend.

Mojo con Tomate (Tomato Mojo Sauce)

Use as a base for cooking beans or meat, or as a topping on cooked eggs or rice.

Makes about 2 cups (475 ml)

- ¼ cup (60 ml) olive oil
- 1 white onion, minced
- ½ bell pepper, deveined and minced
- 3 garlic cloves, minced
- ½ cup (120 ml) tomato paste
- ½ cup (120 ml) water
- 2 tsp white vinegar
- ½ tsp ground cumin
- Salt to taste

Heat olive oil in pan over medium heat then add onion and pepper. Cook until soft; add garlic and cook for another minute. Add the remaining ingredients and simmer over low heat for 6–8 mins.

Aceite de Achiote (Annatto Oil)

Annatto seeds, which grow in pods on a tree, have a very mild flavor and are most often used as an oil or paste to add color to a dish— the clay-red seeds lend a golden hue when mixed with foods. Achiote is also known as "bija."

Makes about ½ cup (120 ml)

- ½ cup (120 ml) olive oil
- ¼ cup (40 g) annatto seeds

Combine oil and annatto seeds in a saucepan and warm over medium-low heat, stirring constantly, until the oil has turned a rich orange color, 4–6 mins. Cool. Strain, discard seeds, and store oil in a glass jar for later use.

Chef Solo Chef Binimelis Sami Carol Meraldo

PLATOS PRINCIPALES

Pollo • Chicken

- Pollo al Ajillo (Garlic Chicken) page 19
- Pollo Asado Relleno de Moros
  (Roast Chicken Stuffed with Rice & Beans) page 20
- Fricasé de Pollo (Chicken Fricassee) page 22
- Pollo con Piña (Chicken with Pineapple) page 23
- Bocaditos (Pepper Paste, or Pepper Spread, Chicken &
  Pork Mousse) page 28
- Caldos (Chicken, Meat, or Seafood Stock) page 30

Puerco • Pork

- Lechón Asado (Roast Pork Shoulder) page 24
- Ajiaco (Classic Cuban Stew) page 26
- Masitas de Puerco: Dos Formas
  (Fried Pork Bites: 2 Ways) page 27
- Chuletas Ahumadas con Piña (Smoked Pork Chops
  with Pineapple) page 29
- Caldo Gallego (Galician-Style Soup) page 40

Lázaro Idaliana

Res • Beef

- Boliche (Stewed Stuffed Beef) page 32
- Ropa Vieja (Stewed Shredded Beef) page 34
- Carne con Papas (Beef & Potato Stew) page 35
- Bistec de Palomilla (Beef Cutlet with Onions) page 36
- Vaca Frita (Fried Shredded Beef) page 37
- Picadillo (Spiced Ground Beef) page 38
- Rabo Encendido (Stewed Oxtail) page 39

Maria Isabel

Chivo • Goat

- Chivo de Chilindrón (Stewed Goat) page 41

Cocinando con Cubanos
Cooking with Cubans

During my first trip to Cuba, I stayed in a *casa particular* (private home), rented to me by a neighboring family. I cooked in the kitchen of this apartment almost every day for a month, working side by side with professional chefs, mothers young and old, and even my landlords, as we prepared dozens of Cuban main dishes, sides, and desserts. We made family-size portions, 2 to 3 recipes at a time. During my stay, I became accustomed to the rhythm of the working-class neighborhood, even when I was home, for all the street sounds and smells entered my 3rd-floor apartment through the slatted wood windows. Every day, I heard the calls of vendors selling things like brooms, sweets, and mattress stuffing, and smelled everything from car exhaust to the freshly baked *empanadas*. These sights, sounds, and smells quickly became the backdrop to my time in central Havana. We made *torrejas en almíbar* (sweet Cuban toast), *fricasé de pollo* (chicken fricassee), and so many other dishes to the hustle-and-bustle soundtrack of life in the city.

I gained a much broader perspective of Cuban culture when, months later, I traveled to the east coast of the country. This region has more differences than I can count, and the cuisine reflects them: the freshly made chocolate, the sweet and savory dishes made with fresh coconut, and the seafood—oh, the seafood! I loved the simply prepared lobster tails and coconut shrimp that I encountered there. And thanks to chefs in the cities of Guantánamo, Baracoa, Holguín, and Gibara, I was introduced to such dishes as *chivo de chilindrón* (stewed goat) and *jaiba rellena,* (stuffed crab shells). Although many Cubans cook using imported foods and convenience ingredients (chicken shipped from overseas and seasoning packets, for example), they demonstrate a real pride in using ingredients from their area when they can. One afternoon I visited Alberto Gámez Ronda on the beach of Gibara as he prepared a lunch of battered fish, plantains, and *ensalada mixta* of cucumbers and string beans.

He explained something that stuck with me: Making a dish using the same ingredients and in the same way as one's grandparents is a way to keep rituals alive. That he told me this as he whipped up lunch just feet from the ocean in the simplest of kitchens perhaps had its own impact, but still, I couldn't agree more.

alberto

Maria

Pedro

my CUBAN KITCHEN in Havana

 ≡ Key

1. Cafetera Moka (Espresso Maker)
2. Olla de Presión (Pressure Cooker)
3. Otra Olla de Presión (Another Pressure Cooker)
4. Cuchillo (Knife)
5. La Cuchara Mamá (The Big Mama Spoon)
6. Platos (Dishes)
7. Aceite (Oil)
8. Vino Seco (Dry White Wine)

9. Especias (Spices)
10. Ventilador (Fan)
11. Tazas para Espresso (Espresso Cups)
12. Caldero de Hierro (Cast-Iron Pot)
13. Trenza de Cebollas (Braid of Onions)
14. La Mesa del Comedor (Dining Room Table)
15. Mejor Lugar para Reposar y Tomar Fotos de la Cocina (Best Place to Stand and Take Photos of Cooking)

16. Refrigerador en Sala (Refrigerator in Living Room)
17. Calentador de Agua Eléctrico (Electric Water Heater)
18. La Estufa Chiquita (The Little Stove)

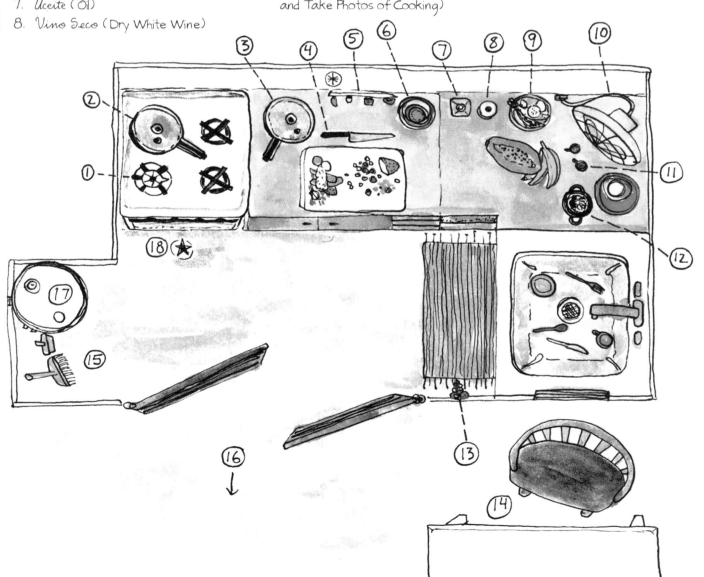

pollo al AJILLO

Garlic Chicken

Serves 6

- 6 garlic cloves, minced
- 1 tsp salt
- ¼ cup (60 ml) lime juice
- ½ cup (120 ml) olive oil, divided
- 3 lb (1.4 kg) chicken breasts
- 1 onion, chopped
- ½ cup (120 ml) vino seco (dry white wine)

Simple to make, pollo al ajillo travels well & leftovers are delicious tucked into a sandwich on Cuban bread.

Using a mortar and pestle, mash the garlic and salt together to make a paste. Stir in the lime juice and ¼ cup (60 ml) olive oil.

Put the chicken in a glass bowl and rub the marinade all over the meat. Cover and refrigerate at least 3 hours, but preferably overnight.

Heat the remaining ¼ cup (60 ml) olive oil in a large skillet over medium heat. Reserving the marinade, transfer chicken to the skillet and brown on both sides. Add onions, reduce heat, and cook for 15–20 mins. Add the wine and the reserved marinade and cook, uncovered, until tender, 10–15 mins. Serve over rice with Mariquitas (page 81).

POLLO asado RELLENO de MOROS

Roast Chicken Stuffed with Rice & Beans

This is a great dish to make with leftover rice and beans, or prepare them ahead to save time. The flavor will improve if you marinate the chicken for 6-8 hours or overnight. Note: Many Cubans refer to the classic dish of rice and beans as simply moros (beans).

Serves 6

Ingredients:

1 large or 2 small whole chickens (total of 5–6 lb/2.3–2.7 kg)

1 lime or lemon, halved

2 garlic cloves

1 tsp salt

½ cup (120 ml) olive oil, divided

¼ cup (60 ml) sour orange juice
   (or equal parts lime and orange juice)

½ tsp cumin

½ tsp oregano

½ tsp black pepper

4 cups (1 kg) Congrí (page 55)

2 Tbsp softened butter

Rinse the chicken and pat dry. Rub the halved lime all over it.

Using a mortar and pestle, crush the garlic and salt to form a paste. Stir in ¼ cup (60 ml) olive oil, the sour orange juice, cumin, oregano, and black pepper.

With your fingers, gently separate the skin from the breast meat, taking care not to rip the skin. Spoon some of the marinade between the skin and the breast. Rub the rest of the marinade all over the chicken, including the cavity. Cover and refrigerate overnight.

Preheat oven to 450°F (232°C). Transfer the chicken to a roasting pan and fill its cavity with the rice and beans. Combine the butter and remaining ¼ cup (60 ml) olive oil and rub over the chicken. Pour any remaining marinade over the chicken. Tuck wings under the bird and tie its legs.

Roast in the oven for 10–15 minutes. Reduce the temperature to 350°F (177°C) and roast for 20 minutes per lb, basting occasionally. Chicken is ready when a meat thermometer inserted into the thigh reads 165°F (74°C). Remove from the oven and scoop out the rice and beans; serve in a separate bowl. Let the chicken rest before carving. Enjoy with Col Salteada (Sautéed Cabbage), page 93.

21

Fricasé de POLLO

Chicken Fricassee

Serves 6

The ingredients for this dish have a strong Spanish influence: dry white wine, tomato paste, and alcaparrado, which can be purchased in a jar in the Spanish section of the grocery store. You can make your own by mixing olives, pimento strips, and capers in brine.

- ¼ cup (60 ml) olive oil
- 1 whole chicken, cut into 8 pieces and skinned
- Salt to taste
- 1 large onion, diced
- 1 small red bell pepper, sliced
- 1 small green bell pepper, sliced
- 3 garlic cloves
- 1½ cups (350 ml) dry white wine
- 1 jar (8 oz/230 g) alcaparrado, including brine (substitute ¾ cup/106 g pimento stuffed green olives & ¼ cup/30 g capers)
- 1 can (6 oz/180 ml) tomato paste
- ¼ cup (38 g) golden raisins
- 4 whole culantro leaves or ½ cup (50 g) chopped cilantro stems in large spice ball
- ½ tsp achiote (annatto), ground
- ½ tsp cumin
- ½ tsp curry powder
- 1 cup (240 ml) water, or as needed
- 4 medium potatoes, quartered
- 8 Tostones (see page 82), optional*

Heat the olive oil in a large pot over medium-high heat and brown chicken on all sides, adding a little salt as you do this. Add onions, peppers, and a little more oil if needed. Sauté until vegetables are softened, about 10 mins, then add garlic and cook for 2 mins more. Stir in the wine, alcaparrado, tomato paste, raisins, culantro, achiote, cumin, curry, and enough water to almost cover the chicken. Bring to a simmer then lower heat and simmer, covered, until chicken is cooked, 30–45 mins. Add the potatoes and tostones, if using, and cook for another 20 mins until potatoes are tender. Serve over white rice.

*The tostones in the fricassee absorb the juices while maintaining some of their texture. You can also just serve the fried tostones on the side.

Pollo con PIÑA

When Pedro Duperey and I cooked in Martica's big kitchen in Playa, on the outskirts of Havana, we'd always began by taking off our street shoes and putting on flip-flops. To remove shoes after grocery shopping in the bustling city center on a hot afternoon was one of those things that always lent a sense of relief. In this case, the ritual of slipping on Martica's sandals was also motivation to begin cooking! Salsa music always played in the background, and we'd prepare a big meal for the family while sipping rum cocktails. This is one of Pedro's favorites.

CHICKEN WITH PINEAPPLE • SERVES 6

Ingredients:

3–4 garlic cloves
1 Tbsp salt, plus more for seasoning
3 limes
3 Tbsp white vinegar, divided
1 red onion, minced, divided
½ cup (120 ml) vegetable oil, divided
1 whole chicken, cut into 8 pieces

1 pineapple, cut into bite-size pieces (page 102)
2 Tbsp sugar
2 cups (475 ml) water
1 green bell pepper, sliced
6 oz (180 ml) tomato paste
¼ cup (28 g) cornstarch
Pepper

▷ Using a mortar and pestle, mash together garlic and 1 Tbsp salt to a paste. Stir in the juice of 2 limes, 2 Tbsp vinegar, half of the minced onion, and ¼ cup (60 ml) vegetable oil. Marinate the chicken for at least 30 mins in this mixture.

▷ Heat the remaining ¼ cup (60 ml) oil in a skillet over medium heat. Brown the chicken all over, then pour in the remaining marinade.

▷ Stir in the pineapple, sugar, water, and a pinch of salt. Add the bell pepper, remaining onion and tomato paste and mix well. Simmer for 30–40 mins over low heat.

▷ Remove ½ cup (120 ml) of the simmering liquid and mix it with the cornstarch. Pour this mixture back into the pan and simmer for a few more minutes to thicken the sauce.

▷ Season the dish with the juice of 1 lime, the remaining 1 Tbsp vinegar, and salt and pepper to taste.

¡La FIESTA Cubana!

When Cubans celebrate festive occasions, it's customary to roast a whole pig on a spit or in a caja de China (Chinese box)—a type of grill where the pig is sandwiched between two metal grates and flipped halfway through cooking. For a smaller gathering, lechón asado does the trick.

LECHÓN ASADO

ROAST PORK SHOULDER • Serves 10–12

- 7–8 lb (3.2–3.6 kg) bone-in pork shoulder
- 5 garlic cloves
- 2 Tbsp salt
- 1 cup (240 ml) sour orange juice (or ½ cup (120 ml) orange juice and ½ cup (120 ml) lime juice)
- 1 Tbsp cumin
- 1 tsp dried oregano

1. Trim fat from pork shoulder. Score skin in a crisscross pattern, partly detaching it from the meat to make space for the marinade. With a sharp knife, make 1-inch (2.5-cm) deep slits all over the meat. Place in a Dutch oven and set aside.

2. MOJO: With a mortar and pestle, crush the garlic and salt to make a coarse paste. Stir in the orange juice, cumin, and oregano. Pour mojo over the pork shoulder and into the slits. Cover and refrigerate at least 10 hours.

3. Remove pork from fridge and let sit at room temperature for 30–40 mins. Heat oven to 500°F (260°C).

4. Cover pot and place in the oven. Lower temperature to 300°F (149°C) and cook for 3 hours. Remove lid and cook for 2 hours more, basting the meat every 30 mins. Increase oven temperature to 425°F (218 C) and roast a few minutes more until the skin is crisp.

5. Remove from the oven and let stand for at least 15 mins before serving.

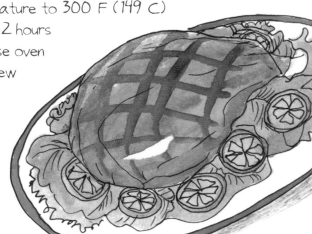

Serve with Congrí (page 55) and Yuca con Mojo (page 87).

Ajiaco

Serves 10–12 *Classic Cuban Stew*

Considered the national dish of Cuba, ajiaco dates back to the 1500s, making it one of the island's oldest recipes. This thick stew of meat and viandas (starches) truly reflects the idea of comida criolla: a fusion of Spanish, African, and native Cuban ingredients. Also referred to as caldosa, this recipe serves a crowd!

- ½ lb (230 g) tasajo (dehydrated beef, similar to beef jerky; optional), cut into 3-inch (7.5-cm) strips
- 1 whole chicken, cut into 8 pieces
- 12 cups (3 L) water
- 1 lb (450 g) pork loin, fat trimmed, cut into 1-inch (2.5-cm) cubes
- 1 lb (450 g) skirt steak, cut into 3-inch (7.5-cm) strips
- 1 lb (450 g) malanga, peeled and cut into 1-inch (2.5-cm) pieces
- ½ lb (230 g) ñame (yam, page 78) (optional), peeled and cut into 1-inch (2.5-cm) pieces

- 1 green plantain, peeled and cut into 1-inch (2.5-cm) rounds
- 1 ripe plantain, peeled and cut into 1-inch (2.5-cm) rounds
- 1 lb (450 g) fresh or frozen yuca (if fresh, peel and quarter lengthwise)
- 1 lb (450 g) yams, peeled and cut into 1-inch (2.5-cm) pieces
- 1 boniato, peeled and cut into 1-inch (2.5-cm) pieces
- 1½ lb (675 g) kabocha squash, seeded, peeled and cut into 2-inch (5-cm) cubes
- 2 ears of corn, cut into 3-inch (7.5-cm) rounds
- 4 limes, cut into wedges

Sofrito:

- ¼ cup (60 ml) olive oil
- 2 large onions, chopped
- 2 large green bell peppers, cored and chopped
- 8 garlic cloves, minced
- 1 Tbsp cumin

- 8 whole culantro leaves (or 20 sprigs cilantro)
- 1 cup (240 ml) tomato sauce
- 2 Tbsp salt

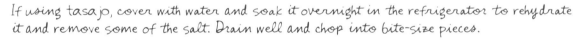

If using tasajo, cover with water and soak it overnight in the refrigerator to rehydrate it and remove some of the salt. Drain well and chop into bite-size pieces.

The following day, combine the drained tasajo, chicken, and water in a large pot and bring to a boil. Reduce heat and simmer gently for about 30 mins. Add the pork and steak and cook for 30 mins more. Skim the fat from the top of the stock.

Meanwhile, make the sofrito: Heat the olive oil in a skillet over medium heat. Add the onions and peppers and cook, stirring occasionally, until softened, 8–10 mins. Add the garlic, cumin, culantro, tomato sauce, and salt and cook until flavors meld, about 10 mins. Set aside.

Add all the vegetables, except the corn, to the meat mixture. Stir in the sofrito and the juice of 1 lime and cook until the vegetables are tender, about 45 mins. Add the corn and simmer for 15–20 mins more. Serve with remaining lime wedges.

MASITAS

DE PUERCO: *dos formas*

FRIED PORK BITES: 2 WAYS • SERVES 4—6

*Although it may seem counterintuitive to mix oil
and water, this technique is a common
way to tenderize cuts of meat.*

First Method:

- 3 garlic cloves
- 2 tsp salt
- 1 cup (240 ml) sour orange juice
- 3 lb (1.4 kg) boneless pork loin, cut into 2-inch (5-cm) cubes
- 1 cup (240 ml) vegetable oil or lard
- ½ cup (120 ml) water
- 1 onion, sliced or diced
- Lime wedges, for serving

Using a mortar and pestle, mash the garlic and salt together into a paste. Transfer to a glass bowl and stir in the sour orange juice. Add the pork and toss to coat with the marinade. Cover and refrigerate overnight.

Combine the oil and water in a deep Dutch oven. Add the pork with its marinade and cook, uncovered, over medium-low heat until the water evaporates, 30—45 mins. When the water has evaporated completely, continue to cook the pork until it is evenly brown but still tender. Add the onions and fry until crispy. Serve with *Yuca con Mojo* (page 87; pour the mojo from the meat over it) and *Congrí* (page 55), and garnish with lime wedges.

Second Method:

- 3 lbs (1.4 kg) boneless pork loin, cut into 2-inch (5-cm) cubes
- 2 tsp salt
- 1 cup (240 ml) vegetable oil or lard
- 1 cup (240 ml) water
- 1 onion, diced
- 2 garlic cloves, crushed
- Juice of 1 lime

Season the pork with the salt. Combine the pork, oil, and water in a Dutch oven. Cook over medium-high heat until the water evaporates, 30—45 mins. Once the water has evaporated, continue to cook the pork until browned then add the onions and fry until crispy. Using a slotted spoon, remove the pork and onions from the pan. Add the crushed garlic and cook 1—2 mins, until golden, then add the lime juice. Pour the sauce on the meat and serve over rice.

BOCADITOS

These two spreads are great to serve at a party as a finger food, or for an appetizer at a multicourse dinner. For the mousse, you can replace the chicken with cooked ham or use a mixture of equal parts chicken and ham, as Maria Gonzalez suggested to me. The pepper spread, based on a recipe by Adelliala Bestard Moya, is a downright delicious option to serve with the mousse or even solo as a vegetarian appetizer.

Pasta de Pimento
Pepper Paste

- 3 red bell peppers
- 1 onion, diced
- 1 Tbsp olive oil
- 1 cup (240 ml) tomato purée
- 1 Tbsp flour
- Salt to taste
- 2 Tbsp vinegar
- 1 egg
- 3 garlic cloves

Add all ingredients to the food processor and process until smooth. Then pass the mixture through a colander, separating the pepper peels. Add to a saucepan and heat over medium-low; stir for 3—5 mins to thicken. Serve with toasted bread or celery and carrot sticks.

Mousse de Pollo y Cerdo
Chicken and Pork Mousse

- 8 oz (230 g) cooked boneless chicken or smoked ham
- 8 oz (230 g) cream cheese
- 1 cup (340 g) roasted red peppers
- 1 Tbsp chopped sweet pickles
- 2 Tbsp mayonnaise
- ½ tsp Tabasco sauce
- ¼ tsp salt

Combine all ingredients in a food processor and process until smooth. To serve, spread the mousse on saltines, thin slices of bread, or inside small rolls.

Chuletas Ahumadas con Piña

Smoked Pork Chops with Pineapple

SERVES 6

Smoking has always been a common preservation method in Cuba, and the process really enhances the flavor of a simple pork chop. The grilled pineapple and honey offers a sweetness that pairs nicely with the pork's smoky flavor.

> ½ cup (120 ml) fresh orange juice
> 3 Tbsp honey
> ½ tsp paprika
> ½ tsp salt

> 4—6 cold-smoked pork chops, about ½-inch (13-mm) thick
> 1 Tbsp butter
> 4—6 slices fresh pineapple
> 3 green onions, finely chopped

1. In a bowl, whisk together the orange juice, honey, paprika, and salt. Add pork chops and refrigerate for 1—2 hrs.

2. Remove pork chops from fridge and blot dry. Reserve marinade.

3. Heat butter in a skillet over medium-high heat. Add pork chops and brown on both sides. Reduce heat and cook until chops are lightly caramelized, about 10 mins. Transfer chops to a platter.

4. Add pineapple to the skillet and cook, flipping once, until caramelized, about 4—6 minutes. Top each pork chop with 1 slice of pineapple and garnish with green onions.

5. Serve with *Congrí* (page 55) and *Plátanos Fritos* (page 80).

CALDOS

Chicken, Meat, or Seafood Stock

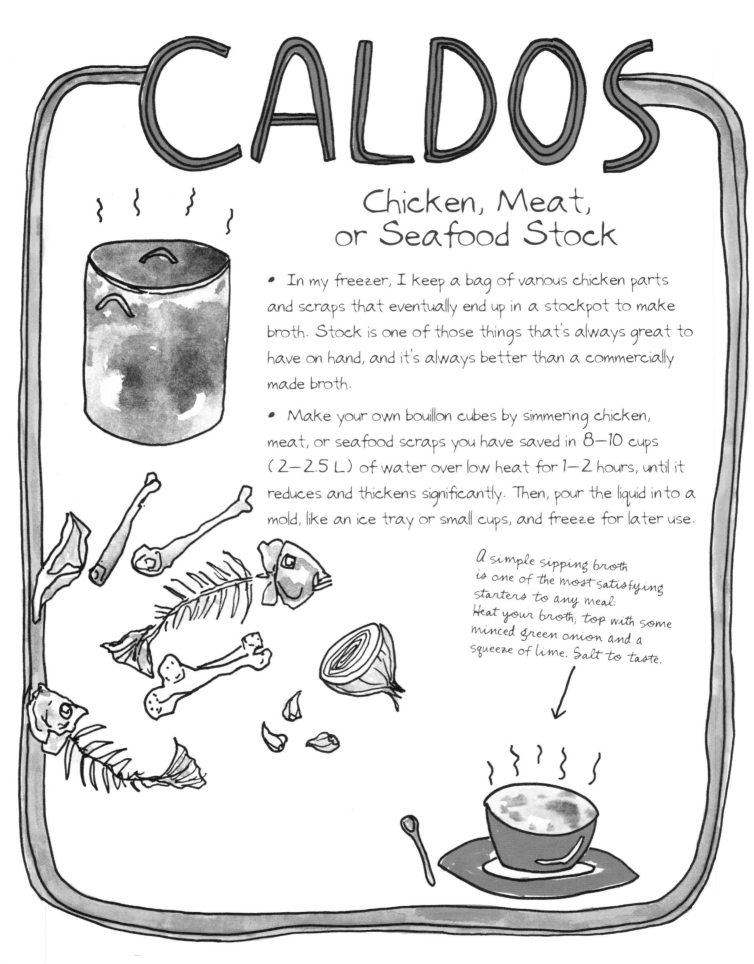

• In my freezer, I keep a bag of various chicken parts and scraps that eventually end up in a stockpot to make broth. Stock is one of those things that's always great to have on hand, and it's always better than a commercially made broth.

• Make your own bouillon cubes by simmering chicken, meat, or seafood scraps you have saved in 8–10 cups (2–2.5 L) of water over low heat for 1–2 hours, until it reduces and thickens significantly. Then, pour the liquid into a mold, like an ice tray or small cups, and freeze for later use.

A simple sipping broth is one of the most satisfying starters to any meal: Heat your broth; top with some minced green onion and a squeeze of lime. Salt to taste.

Res y Vacas en Cuba • Beef & Dairy Cows in Cuba

When I went to Cuba, I soon learned that beef and dairy cattle are not abundant on the island, which is not surprising considering it takes a great deal of resources to raise a cow. The following recipes are traditional, well-loved Cuban dishes, but in my experience, while you will find some beef in restaurants, it is very rare to find it prepared in a Cuban home. Pork is a far more available source of protein, and Cubans use every part of the animal. *Recortado* is the name for all the pork trimmings chopped up, and it's the cheapest type of meat you can find at an outdoor market or *carnicería* (butcher shop).

When I asked people about beef cattle, many recounted the days when Cuba was backed by the USSR. The Soviet Union provided beef cattle to the island, as well as their feed grain. When the USSR collapsed, so did the beef industry, like so many others. Consequently, the island also had to rely more heavily on traditional farming methods, since the oil shortage made it difficult to work the fields using industrial equipment. Draft cattle, or oxen, which had been employed in peasant farming for centuries, became necessary during the 1990s, and they continue to be used to this day.

The dairy products in Cuban supermarkets come from overseas, for the most part; and during my 2016 visit to Havana, it wasn't common to find fresh, locally sourced milk in markets. Most milk available to consumers is powdered. When fresh dairy was available, many people were hesitant to buy it, wary of preservatives added to lengthen its shelf life. I found cheese in the supermarket, mostly Gouda and Swiss, but for the average Cuban it was not affordable. In the coming years it's possible that new trade agreements could help fulfill Cuban consumers' demand for healthy and affordable dairy products; and with time, the local production could grow, too.

BOLICHE

Stewed Stuffed Beef

SERVES 6–8

A Cuban butcher would trim and stuff the meat for you, but I've included instructions for doing it yourself. If you can't find sour oranges, use equal parts orange and lime juice.

- 1 (4-lb/1.8-kg) eye of round roast or beef rump roast, trimmed
- 2 or 3 fresh chorizo links (casing removed)

MOJO

- ½ cup (120 ml) sour orange juice
- 2 garlic cloves, minced
- 2 tsp cumin
- 1 tsp salt

1. With a sharp knife, make a lengthwise slit through the center of the meat. Insert the end of a wooden spoon to expand the opening and make it large enough to stuff. Stuff the chorizo into the opening.

2. To prepare the mojo, whisk together the sour orange juice, garlic, cumin, and salt. Put the beef in a glass baking dish and rub half of the marinade over the beef (reserve the remaining marinade). Cover and refrigerate at least 3 hrs or overnight.

3. To make the sofrito, heat 2 Tbsp olive oil in a large pot over medium heat. Add the onions, bell pepper, and garlic and sauté until soft and golden. Add the tomato paste, cumin, and salt and cook for 1 min more. Scrape the sofrito into a bowl and return the pot to the stove.

SOFRITO

- 4 Tbsp olive oil, divided
- 1 large onion, chopped
- 1 green bell pepper, chopped
- 2 garlic cloves, minced
- 2 Tbsp tomato paste
- 2 tsp cumin
- ½ tsp salt
- 6 culantro leaves (or ½ cup/25 g chopped cilantro), divided
- 1 cup (140 g) pimento-stuffed olives, plus some of the olive juice
- ½ cup (120 ml) vino seco (dry white wine)
- 4 potatoes, peeled and thickly sliced

4. Heat the remaining 2 Tbsp oil in the pot over high heat and brown the meat on all sides. Once the meat has browned, add the remaining marinade, half of the sofrito, 4 culantro leaves, and enough water to come halfway up the meat. Bring to a boil then reduce the heat and simmer, covered tightly, until the meat is tender but not falling apart, 2–3 hrs. Remove the meat from the pot and set aside to cool slightly. Simmer the sauce, uncovered, until slightly reduced. Add the rest of the sofrito, olives, vino seco, and the remaining 2 culantro leaves and cook for about 5 mins.

5. Meanwhile, cut the meat into ½-inch (13-mm) thick slices. Arrange the potatoes along the bottom of the pot in the sauce. Place the meat over potatoes and cover with sauce. Cook, covered, over medium-low heat until potatoes are tender, 15–20 mins.

6. Remove from the heat and serve the Boliche with Congrí (page 55) or white rice.

Ropa Vieja

STEWED SHREDDED BEEF

SERVES 6-8

Ropa vieja translates to "old clothes," which is appropriate because the meat is first used to make a broth, before getting a second life shredded and seasoned with sofrito, making it "secondhand".

Step 1:

2–3 lb (900–1,350 g) flank steak, cut against the grain into 3-inch (7.5-cm) strips

6 cups (1.5 L) water

1 onion, quartered

3–4 garlic cloves

4 culantro leaves or ½ cup (25 g) whole cilantro sprigs

1 bay leaf

Step 2:

¼ cup (60 ml) olive oil

1 green bell pepper, sliced

1 red bell pepper, sliced

1 onion, sliced

3 garlic cloves, minced

2 tsp cumin

2 tsp Spanish paprika

½ cup (120 ml) vino seco (dry white wine)

3 Tbsp tomato paste

4 leaves culantro or ¼ cup (15 g) chopped cilantro

2 tsp white vinegar

2 tsp salt

White rice, for serving

Step 1: To make the broth, place the meat in a large heavy pot and cover it with water. Add the quartered onion, garlic cloves, and bay leaf. Bring to a boil over high heat, then reduce the heat and simmer, covered for 2 hrs, until the beef is very tender. Remove the beef from the stock and set aside to cool. (Save the stock for another use.*) When the meat is cool enough to handle, use two forks to shred it.

It is also possible to use a pressure cooker for this first part of the preparation. Bring cooker up to pressure and cook for 15–20 mins. Release the pressure using the quick release valve according to the manufacturer's directions.

Step 2: Heat the olive oil in a large skillet over medium heat. Add the bell peppers, onions, and garlic and cook, stirring occasionally, until softened and lightly browned, 6–8 mins. Stir in the cumin and paprika then add the wine, tomato paste, culantro, vinegar, and 1½ cups (350 ml) of the reserved broth. Simmer for about 10 mins. Stir in the shredded meat and the salt and cook gently for 20 mins more. Serve with white rice, Plátanos Fritos (page 80) and La Ensalada Mixta (page 95).

*Save the remaining broth for making one of the bean soups, such Caldo Gallego (page 40).

CARNE con PAPAS

La libreta

Beef & Potato Stew · Serves 8

In contrast to most starchy tubers (like yuca), which are available year round in Cuba, potatoes are available for only a few months. When in season, they're a favorite addition to the monthly food rations. I witnessed lines of people at the ration distribution center near my apartment in Havana, ready to pick up their potatoes, all with their libretas in hand—the notebooks that record the monthly allotment of goods provided by the government. This recipe was one of the dishes we made during potato season. Hearty, filling, substantial, and economical, Carne con Papas is comfort food in its purest form.

- 3 lb (1.4 kg) beef top round or boneless pork shoulder cut into 1½-inch (4-cm) cubes
- Salt and pepper
- ¼ cup (60 ml) olive oil
- 1 large onion, chopped
- 2 ají cachucha, seeded and minced, or 1 green bell pepper, cored and chopped
- 3 garlic cloves, minced
- 1 Tbsp paprika
- 1½ tsp cumin
- ¼ tsp achiote (optional)
- 1 cup (240 ml) vino seco (dry white wine)
- 1 cup (240 ml) beef broth
- 1 cup (200 g) canned diced tomatoes
- 2 Tbsp tomato paste
- 4 whole culantro leaves or ¼ cup (15 g) chopped cilantro
- 4 red or Yukon gold potatoes, peeled and cut into 1-inch (2.5-cm) cubes
- 3 carrots, cut into ½-inch (13-mm) rounds
- White rice, for serving

Season the meat with salt and pepper. Heat the oil in a large pan over medium-high heat. Working in batches, pan fry the beef on all sides, transferring to a bowl when browned. Add the onions, peppers, and garlic and cook, stirring occasionally, until soft, 5—7 mins. Add the paprika, cumin, and achiote, and cook for about 1 min. Return the beef to the pan, along with the wine, broth, tomatoes, tomato paste, and culantro. Bring to a boil, then reduce the heat to a simmer. Cover and cook, stirring every 20 mins, until meat is tender, 1—2 hrs. Add the potatoes and carrots and cook until tender, about 30 mins more. Serve over white rice.

Bistec de Palomilla

Serves 4-6

Beef Cutlet with Onions

A Cuban classic, found on many restaurant menus. Try this recipe as a sandwich, pan con bistec, on Cuban bread with onions, lettuce and tomato.

> 1½ lb (775 g) top round or sirloin steak
> 3 garlic cloves
> ½ tsp salt

> ¼ cup (60 ml) vegetable oil
> 1 onion, sliced
> Juice of 1 lime, plus 1 lime cut into wedges

① Cut the steak into 4 pieces and pound to about ¼-inch (6-mm) thick. Place in a glass container.

② Using a mortar and pestle, combine the garlic and salt to make a coarse paste. Spread the paste over the steak. Cover and refrigerate for at least 30 mins.

③ Heat the oil in a frying pan over medium-high heat and fry steaks, 2 at a time, about 2 mins per side. Transfer to a serving platter and cover to keep hot. Repeat with the remaining steaks, replenishing oil if needed.

④ After all steaks are cooked, add any remaining garlic paste to the skillet. Bring to a simmer, then add the sliced onions, cover, and cook until lightly cooked but still crunchy, 1-3 mins. Stir in the lime juice to deglaze the pan then pour onions and pan juices over the steaks. Garnish with lime wedges.

⑤ Serve with white rice, black beans, and Plátanos Fritos (page 80) or a fried egg.

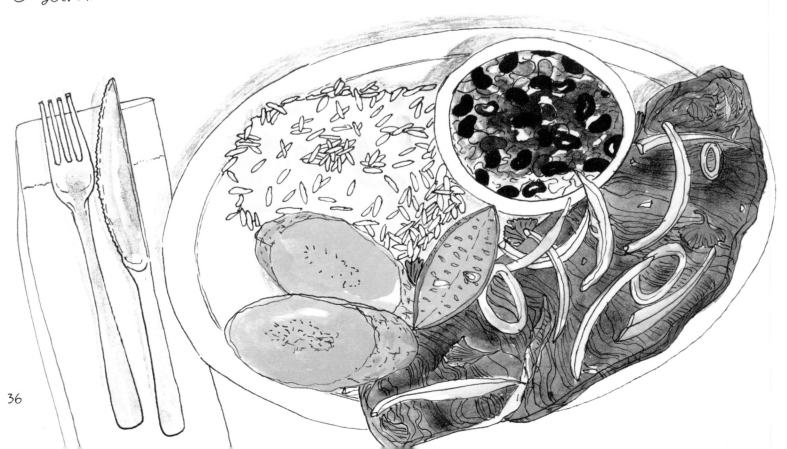

Vaca Frita

FRIED SHREDDED BEEF
SERVES 6-8

This tender, shredded beef is a home-cooked classic—definitely not a fancy meal, but oh, so satisfying! Vaca frita means "fried cow": the meat is simmered until it practically falls apart; then it's combined with a citrus marinade, which brightens up the flavors. The trick to achieving the optimal crisp fried texture is to fry the beef in batches, so it doesn't crowd the pan.

Ingredients:

1 recipe Ropa Vieja (page 34)

For the mojo:
2 garlic cloves, minced
½ cup (120 ml) sour orange juice (or equal parts fresh lime and orange juice)
1 tsp salt
¼ cup (60 ml) olive oil, or as needed if frying in batches
1 medium onion, sliced
White rice, for serving
Garnish: minced cilantro, lime wedges

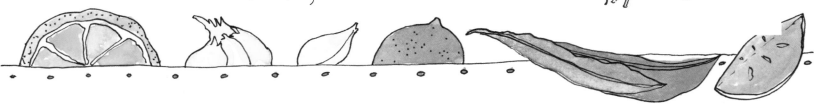

Make the Ropa Vieja according to the instructions on page 34. When the meat is cool enough to handle, use a fork to shred it. Whisk together minced garlic, sour orange juice, and salt in a bowl. Pour mojo over meat and mix with your hands. Let marinate for about 30 mins. Heat olive oil in large skillet over medium heat and sauté the onions until translucent, about 5 mins. Add about half of the beef and fry until onions are soft. Raise heat and fry until the meat is slightly crispy around the edges, then transfer to a serving dish. Repeat with the remaining beef. Serve over white rice garnished with minced cilantro and lime wedges. Enjoy with black beans and plátanos fritos.

PICADILLO

Spiced Ground Beef

RICH, FLAVORFUL, AND VERSATILE, THIS STEWED GROUND BEEF KNOWN AS *picadillo* IS AN ESSENTIAL CUBAN DISH. ENJOY IT AS A FILLING FOR *tostones, pastelitos,* OR *empanadas,* OR ADD POTATOES, CORN, AND RAISINS TO MAKE IT A MAIN DISH.

3 Tbsp olive oil

2 medium onions, diced

1 green bell pepper, cored and diced

1 red bell pepper, cored and diced

2–3 garlic cloves, mashed into a paste

2 tsp cumin

2 tsp paprika

2 tsp salt

2 lb (900 g) lean ground beef

2 cups (480 ml) dry white wine or beer

1 (8-oz) jar alcaparrado or substitute ¾ cup (106 g) green olives and ¼ cup (30 g) capers

¼ cup (60 ml) tomato paste

4 culantro leaves or ½ cup (25 g) chopped cilantro

½ cup (80 g) raisins, preferably golden*

2 cups (350 g) frozen corn*

2 cups (650 g) fried diced potatoes*

• SERVES 4–6 OVER RICE •

FILLS ABOUT 20 *tostones,* OR 15 *empanadas* OR *pastelitos*

Heat the olive oil in a deep frying pan over medium heat. Add the onions, bell peppers, and garlic and cook, stirring occasionally, until onion is translucent, about 5 mins. Stir in the cumin, paprika, and salt and cook for 3 mins more. Add the ground beef, breaking it up with a wooden spoon. Once the beef has browned, let it cook for a few mins more until the extra liquid has evaporated. Add the wine, *alcaparrado,* tomato paste, *culantro,* and raisins. Bring to a boil, reduce the heat, and simmer, partially covered, until reduced by a third, about 45 mins.

Once the *picadillo* has reduced, add the frozen corn and potatoes and cook for an additional 15 mins. Serve over white rice or polenta.

*When making *picadillo* to use as a filling in *Tostones Rellenos* (page 83) or *Empanadas* (page 116), omit the raisins, corn, and potatoes.

Rabo Encendido

Stewed Oxtail • Serves 6

This dish is more mildly spiced than many other Caribbean oxtail recipes, but includes a similarly rich and satisfying gravy. Make sure to ask your butcher for large, meaty pieces of oxtail.

1 cup (240 ml) red wine

¼ cup (60 ml) + 4 tsp olive oil, divided

1 tsp salt, divided

2 pounds (900 g) oxtail, sliced

Flour, for dredging

1 medium onion, chopped

1 green bell pepper, chopped

½ red bell pepper, chopped

1½ lb (1.1 kg) potatoes, cut into ½-inch (13-mm) dice

1 carrot, cut into ½-inch (13-mm) thick slices

1–2 garlic cloves

1 (15-oz/420-g) can tomato sauce

1 cup (240 ml) beef broth

2 bay leaves

½ tsp freshly ground nutmeg

¼ tsp ground allspice

1. Whisk together ½ cup (120 ml) red wine, 2 tsp oil, and ½ tsp salt in a bowl. Add the oxtails and refrigerate overnight.

2. Drain meat, reserving marinade. Lightly dredge the oxtails with flour. Heat ¼ cup (60 ml) oil in a heavy pot or Dutch oven over medium heat and brown meat on all sides, working in batches if necessary so as not to crowd the pot. Transfer meat to a bowl.

3. Add 2 tsp oil and the reserved marinade, stirring to deglaze the pot. Add onions and peppers and sauté until soft. Add potatoes and carrots and cook until potatoes are done, but still firm, adding more olive oil if necessary.

4. Mash garlic together with ½ tsp salt with a mortar and pestle; add to the vegetables and cook for another minute.

5. Return the oxtails and any juices to the pot, along with the tomato sauce, broth, bay leaves, nutmeg, and allspice. Bring to a boil, reduce heat to low, and simmer, covered, until the meat is fork tender, about 2 hrs.

6. Remove bay leaves; serve over white rice.

CALDO GALLEGO

GALICIAN-STYLE SOUP • Serves 6

This hearty stew comes directly from the immigrants who arrived in Cuba from northern Spain at the turn of the 20th century. The heartiness of the smoked pork and spiced sausage combined with the delicate white beans and leafy greens lend a nice, varied texture to this dish. It's extra-satisfying scooped up with a slice of crusty bread!

- 1 lb (450 g) dried white beans, such as cannellini or great northern
- 8 oz (230 g) fatback bacon or salt pork, cut into 1-inch (2.5-cm) pieces
- 8 oz (230 g) smoked ham shank, cut into 2-inch (5-cm) pieces
- 8 oz (230 g) chorizo, casing removed and cut into ½-inch (13-mm) rounds
- 1 large onion, chopped
- 1 green bell pepper, chopped
- 4 garlic cloves, minced
- 8 cups (950 ml) chicken stock or water

- 2 bay leaves
- 1 lb (450 g) red potatoes, peeled and cut into 1-inch (2.5-cm) dice
- 1 medium turnip, peeled and cut into ½-inch (13-mm) dice
- 3 cups (90 g) chopped acelgas (Swiss chard) or collard greens
- Salt and pepper

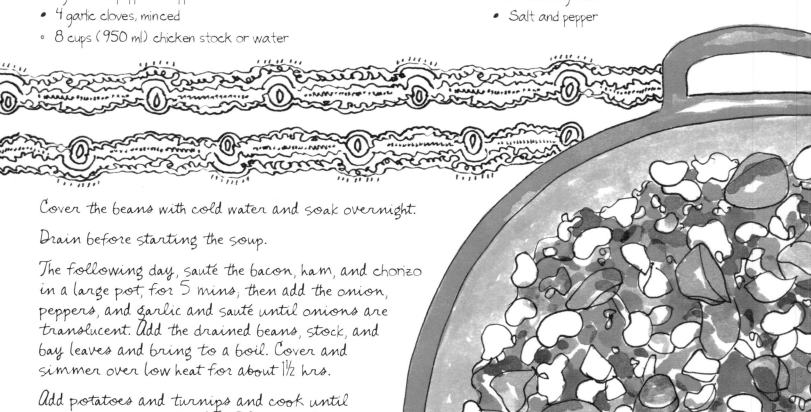

Cover the beans with cold water and soak overnight. Drain before starting the soup.

The following day, sauté the bacon, ham, and chorizo in a large pot, for 5 mins; then add the onion, peppers, and garlic and sauté until onions are translucent. Add the drained beans, stock, and bay leaves and bring to a boil. Cover and simmer over low heat for about 1½ hrs.

Add potatoes and turnips and cook until vegetables are tender, 15–20 mins. Stir in greens and cook until wilted, 5–10 mins. Season with salt and pepper to taste. Serve with white crusty bread.

When I visited the city of Guantánamo, I headed to Artechef, a restaurant-bar and cooking school that serves as the city's chapter of the Asociación Culinaria. There, the kitchen staff prepared the best Chivo de Chilindrón I'd had yet. The dish is recreated here, including chile guaguao (little spicy peppers; page 14). When making goat stew, the meat must be tender—plan to cook the chilindrón slowly until the meat falls off the bone, at least a couple of hours. Pro tip: Use a pressure cooker (page 49) to shorten the cooking time.

especial ahora : STEWED GOAT
CHIVO de CHILINDRÓN
Serves 6

Marinade:

- Juice of 2 sour oranges,
  or juice of 1 lime and 1 orange
- 4 garlic cloves, minced
- ½ tsp chopped fresh oregano
- ½ tsp cumin
- 1 Tbsp salt
- ½ tsp pepper
- 3 lb (1.4 kg) bone-in goat,
  cut into 3–4-inch (7.5–10-cm) pieces

Chilindrón:

- ½ cup (120 ml) olive oil
- 2 onions, chopped
- 1 bell pepper, diced
- 6–8 dried or fresh chile guaguao
  or spicy pepper of choice
- 3 garlic cloves, minced
- ½ cup (120 ml) tomato paste
- ¼ cup (60 ml) white vinegar
- 2 whole culantro leaves
  or ¼ cup (15 g) cilantro, chopped
- ½ tsp cumin
- ½ tsp minced fresh oregano
- Salt and pepper

① The night before, combine the sour orange juice, garlic, oregano, cumin, 1 Tbsp salt and ½ tsp pepper. Add the goat meat and toss to coat. Cover and refrigerate overnight to marinate.

② Heat oil in a large heavy cooking pot over medium heat, then make the sofrito: add the onions, peppers, chiles, and garlic and sauté until soft. Add the meat and cook for 5–7 mins. Stir in the tomato paste, vinegar, culantro, cumin, and oregano. Reduce heat and simmer, covered, until the meat is very tender, about 2 hrs. Season to taste with salt and pepper.

③ If using a pressure cooker, sauté vegetables as directed then add the remaining ingredients, seal the pressure cooker, and cook on high pressure until meat is tender, 30–35 mins.

④ For a true eastern Cuba feast, serve with Congrí (page 55) or Tamales de Maíz (page 60) with fresh papaya and cheese for dessert!

RICE, BEANS & CORN

Arroz • Rice

Frijoles • Beans

Maíz • Corn

Nitza Villapol y la Cocina Cubana

Nitza Villapol and Cuban Cuisine

If there is a mother of Cuban cuisine, it's Nitza Villapol. Most every Cuban will tell you that Nitza wrote the book when it comes to Cuban Criolla classics. She was famous for hosting a cooking show on Cuban television called *Cocina al Minuto*, which first aired in 1951 and lasted for more than 46 years. Many Cubans remember sitting around the television on Sundays to watch Nitza's cooking show, which was broadcast live each week at 11:45 a.m. By the 1950s, Nitza was famous not only for her television broadcasts, but for her books, *Cocina Criolla* (1954) and *Cocina al Minuto* (1958).

Born in New York City to Cuban immigrant parents, Nitza and her family moved back to Cuba when she was nine. She studied nutrition in London during World War II, which gave her a foundation for health-conscious meals.

Nitza continued to be a strong supporter of the Cuban revolution throughout her life. Resources were hard to come by at times, so Nitza devised alternative methods of preparation for countless recipes. With the help of her longtime assistant, Margot Bacallao, she shared her keen sense of creativity in the kitchen, on television, and in print.

Sometimes her menu plan for the cooking show was not finalized until minutes before her broadcast, due to the limited rations and food shortages at various times throughout the revolution, most notably during the economic crises of the 1990s (known as the *Período Especial*/Special Period). She famously taught her viewers how to fry an egg without oil and how to make flan with only 1 egg. Nitza also consistently educated people about the benefits of including more vegetables, less fat, and less meat in their diets.

During my cooking experience in Cuba, I saw many cherished copies of Nitza's cookbooks; nearly all of my collaborators owned them, both of which are now out of print in Cuba. All were tattered, splattered, and falling apart at the binding—evidence of how much their owners valued her cookbooks.

"La Cocina es un Arte, un arte de cada pueblo, un arte menor que forma parte de la Cultura de los pueblos"

— Nitza Villapol

"Cooking is an art, an art of the people, a minor art that forms part of the culture of each region."

— Nitza Villapol

LOS BÁSICOS

At most every Cuban table, white rice is a component of the meal. This foolproof method produces fluffy rice that isn't sticky or dry: the secret is to wash the rice. In a large bowl, wash the rice with cold water. Swish it around with your hand then pour off the cloudy water. Repeat 3–4 times, until the water is clear. Especially in the countryside and smaller towns, cornmeal instead of rice might complement a main dish. Field corn is ground fresh and then dried to make *harina de maíz*. Any protein, stews, or black beans could be eaten alongside a portion of *harina de maíz*.

ARROZ Blanco de Nitza Villapol*

White Rice • Adapted from Nitza's cookbook *Cocina al Minuto*

Serves 6

3 Tbsp olive oil

2 garlic cloves, mashed

3 cups (700 ml) warm water

1 Tbsp salt

2½ cups (500 g) long-grain white rice, well rinsed and drained

Preparation in a Saucepan:
Heat oil in a saucepan over medium heat, add the garlic cloves and cook until golden, remove. Remove pot from heat to let oil cool, about 2 mins. Add water and salt to the oil, cover and bring to a boil. Add the rinsed and drained rice, cover, and cook over low heat until small air holes appear on surface of rice, 25–30 mins. Remove from heat and let stand for 5 mins before serving.

Preparation in a Pressure Cooker:
Heat oil in a cooker and sauté mashed garlic cloves until golden, then remove. Turn off the heat and let cool for 2 mins, then add water, salt, and rice. Close the pressure cooker and using manufacturer's instructions, bring it up to pressure and cook on high pressure for 3 mins. Release all the pressure as directed by instructions. Open pressure cooker; let stand for 5 mins before serving.

HARINA de Maíz

Cornmeal

Serves 6

1 garlic clove

½ onion, minced

¼ cup (120 ml) butter or olive oil

3 cups (700 ml) water

1 cup (240 ml) milk (or substitute 1 cup water)

1 tsp salt

1 cup (138 g) fine cornmeal

In a saucepan, sauté garlic and onion in butter or olive oil until translucent. Add water, milk, and salt and bring to a boil. While whisking, add the cornmeal and keep whisking as the mixture thickens. Cover the pot and continue to simmer over very low heat for about 10–15 mins, stirring occasionally.

ARROZ con Mariscos

Rice with Seafood

This dish loosely resembles a Spanish paella with its variety of seafood and bright fresh vegetables mixed with rice. It is best served with the day's catch.

Serves 6—8

- ¼ cup (60 ml) olive oil
- 1 large onion, chopped
- 1 green bell pepper, chopped
- 1 red bell pepper, chopped
- 4 garlic cloves, minced
- ½ tsp salt
- 1 tsp Spanish paprika
- 1 tsp cumin
- 3 cups (600 g) white rice
- 3 cups (700 ml) chicken broth
- 1 (12 oz) can of beer

- ½ tsp achiote powder
- Pinch of saffron, optional
- 12 clams
- 2 mussels
- 1 lb (450 g) large raw shrimp, peeled and deveined
- 1 lb (450 g) scallops
- 4 lobster tails, meat removed and cut into bite-size pieces
- 1 cup (134 g) frozen peas
- 1½ lb (230 g) blanched asparagus

Heat the olive oil in a Dutch oven or deep pan over medium heat. Add the onions, bell peppers, and garlic. Cook, stirring occasionally, until onions are translucent, about 8—10 mins. Add the salt, paprika, and cumin, then cook for 1 min more. Stir in the rice and cook for 2 mins. Add the chicken broth, beer, achiote, and saffron, then bring to a boil. Add the seafood, cover, and reduce the heat. Simmer until the rice is tender, but the consistency still moist, about 15 mins. Add frozen peas, cook for 10 more mins. Garnish with blanched asparagus and serve.

ARROZ FRITO

The Chinese-Cuban community is small, but has a long history on the island. There were two waves of migration: The Chinese first came in the 18th century to work the sugarcane fields, and then in the 19th century they migrated from the US to build the railroads. Chinese-Cuban restaurants on the island offer a mix of the two cuisines, and you'll find soy sauce in the pantries of many Cubans. Fried rice is a great main dish to make with leftover rice.

- ½ cup (120 ml) oil
- 4 scallions, chopped
- 3 eggs, beaten
- 1 cup (125 g) chopped cooked pork or chicken
- 1 cup (134 g) frozen peas and carrots
- 1 red bell pepper, thinly sliced
- 4 cups (640 g) cooked rice
- 4 Tbsp soy sauce diluted with 4 Tbsp water
- 1 Tbsp grated fresh ginger (optional)
- 1 cup (134 g) fresh bean sprouts

1. In a large skillet or wok, heat 2 Tbsp of the oil over medium-high heat. Add the scallions and cook for 2-3 mins. Then add the eggs, and let cook, undisturbed, to form a thin omelet. Once omelet is cooked through, remove from pan and set aside.

2. Add remaining oil to pan and stir in the meat, vegetables, and rice. Increase heat slightly and cook until the rice is golden brown and crisp in spots, 5–10 mins. Pour the soy sauce/water mixture over the rice, along with the ginger, if using. Continue cooking, stirring occasionally, until the rice has absorbed all the liquid, 3–5 mins. Stir in bean sprouts. Remove from the heat.

3. Cut the omelet in half and then into thin strips. Garnish each portion of fried rice with the omelet and serve warm.

:ARROZ con POLLO a la CHORRERA:

Cuban-Style Chicken & Rice • Serves 6–8

This Cuban version of chicken with rice was named after the Torreón de la Chorrera, a fortress built by the Spanish settlers in the early 17th century at the mouth of the Almendares River. This principal river that runs through Havana was formerly named La Chorrera, after Amazonian natives who traveled to the Island. It's appropriate that this rice dish has a soupy consistency, since it is named for a waterway.

FOR THE CHICKEN:
- Juice of 1 lemon
- 6 garlic cloves, minced
- 1 tsp fresh oregano, chopped
- ½ tsp cumin
- 1 Tbsp salt
- 1 tsp pepper
- 8–10 chicken thighs

FOR THE RICE:
- ½ cup (120 ml) oil, divided
- 1 large onion, chopped
- 1 large green or red bell pepper, chopped
- 3 large garlic cloves, minced
- 2 dried bay leaves
- ½ tsp pimentón (smoked paprika)
- ¼ tsp ground cumin
- Salt to taste

- 4 oz (120 ml) tomato paste
- 2½ cups (500 g) uncooked white rice
- 2–4 cups (475–900 ml) chicken broth
- 2 Tbsp capers
- ¼ cup (35 g) pitted green olives
- 1 Tbsp fresh oregano, chopped
- 1 (24-oz/700 ml) can of beer
- 1½ cups (200 g) frozen peas, thawed

1. Whisk together lemon juice, garlic, oregano, cumin, salt, and pepper. Add chicken, cover, and marinate for 2–3 hrs in the refrigerator. When ready to cook, remove the chicken and save the marinade for later.

2. Heat ¼ cup (60 ml) oil in a large heavy pan on medium heat. Add the chicken to the pan and cook, flipping halfway through, until golden brown, 4–5 mins on each side. Remove chicken from the pan and set aside.

3. Add the remaining oil to the pan along with the chopped onion, bell pepper, garlic, and bay leaves and sauté over medium heat until soft. Add the paprika, cumin, and salt, then add the tomato paste and the reserved marinade and simmer for 6 mins.

4. Stir in the rice then add 2 cups (475 ml) chicken broth, the capers, green olives, and oregano. Return the chicken to the pan, nestling the pieces into the rice. Add the beer, stir gently, and reduce heat. Simmer, covered, until rice is tender, about 15 mins.

5. This dish is not a soup, but it should have a soupier consistency than a dry rice dish like paella. Add more chicken broth if necessary, then let the dish rest, covered, for 15–20 mins before serving, allowing the rice to plump. Fold in the peas just before serving, so they are bright green and not too soft.

LA OLLA DE PRESIÓN

The Pressure Cooker

In Cuba, pressure cookers are extremely common.
They greatly reduce the use of fuel and electricity in the kitchen,
maximizing time efficiency as well as resources.
Pressure cookers allow people to prepare dishes that traditionally
take hours to make in a fraction of the time. A pressure cooker is a sealed pot.
As it heats, liquid inside it forms steam. The trapped steam increases pressure
in the pot. This raises the boiling point. That means food cooks at a higher
temperature and therefore faster than other methods. There are
both traditional and electric pressure cookers that follow specific methods of
operation; follow manufacturer's directions when using.

- Pressure cookers require liquid to create steam; always cook with at least ½ –1 cup (120 – 240 ml) water.

- Leave at least ⅓ of the space empty to allow the steam to build up and the food, such as beans, to expand as it cooks.

- Allow pressure to build over high heat; lower the heat to maintain the level of pressure.

- Begin timing the recipe when pressure is reached.

- The denser the food, the more time you'll need.

- It's easier to overcook than undercook; always use a timer! Add time in 1–4-minute intervals if you need to cook for longer.

- For consistent results, cut foods into pieces of uniform size to promote even cooking.

- For more flavor, sauté the food first in the pot, deglaze, then pressure-cook.

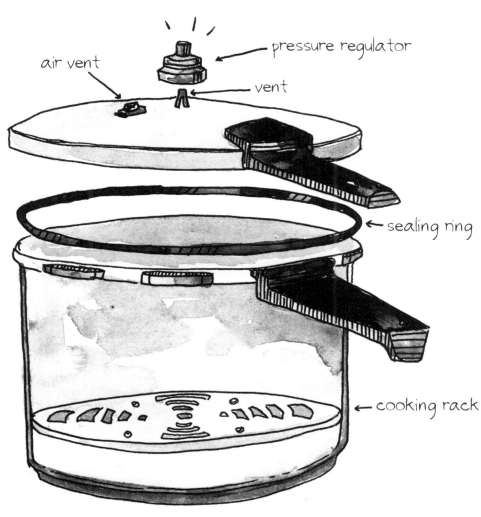

pressure regulator

air vent

vent

sealing ring

cooking rack

Congrí, Moros, Potaje de Colorados

UNDERSTANDING THE TYPES OF BEAN DISHES IN CUBAN CUISINE

Beans have been an essential part of the Cuban diet for hundreds of years. Black beans and red beans, the most prominent varieties in Cuba, nourished the islanders long before the arrival of Christopher Columbus; they were originally brought from South America. It's no wonder; beans are versatile, economical, rich in protein and fiber, and there are infinite ways to prepare them.

Many Cuban cooks are judged by the quality of their bean dishes, whether it's *Congrí* (black beans) or *Moros Colorados* (red beans). It's the *secretos de la cocina* (secrets of the kitchen) that make these simple dishes delicious.

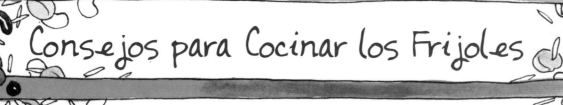

Consejos para Cocinar los Frijoles

TIPS ON COOKING BEANS:

1. Contrary to popular belief, beans do not have to be soaked first. Soaking the beans does not impact their flavor, but does reduce the cooking time significantly (by 40—90 mins, if slow-cooking them and not using a pressure cooker).

2. Cooking times may vary with the type and age of the beans. Beans continue to dry out as they age, meaning they may take longer to cook. Beans are finished cooking when they are tender enough to be mashed easily, but their skins are still intact.

3. Wait to add any acidic ingredients until the beans are fully cooked. Citrus, vinegar, tomatoes, and wine are great flavor enhancers, but will keep the beans from becoming tender if added too early.

4. Adding salt during the cooking process will keep beans from softening. Don't salt the water when you're soaking the beans either.

5. No matter where you purchase your beans, it's always a good idea to pick through and rinse them well before cooking to eliminate any soil or pebbles left over from the harvesting process.

6. If brown foam appears on the surface of the beans while cooking, know this isn't dirt. Just skim it off. Adding a little oil to the beans will prevent foaming.

7. When the room temperature is warm, soak the beans in the refrigerator, so they don't begin to ferment. Signs of fermentation include small bubbles and a slight sour odor.

8. If you have started to soak beans but don't have time to cook them, change the water once a day and keep them in the refrigerator: they'll keep for a few more days.

Potaje de Frijoles Negros

Serves 6 — Stewed Black Beans

The following sequence gives instruction on how to create a simple vegetarian bean dish. From there, I've included some additional methods that build on this recipe. All of these dishes begin with a basic sofrito for cooking the beans. A second round of seasonings and vegetables is added to complete the flavor profile.

For Cooking the Beans:
- 1 lb (450 g) dried black beans
- 1 Tbsp olive oil
- 1 large onion, diced
- 4 garlic cloves, minced
- 4 whole culantro leaves or 3 Tbsp chopped cilantro placed in a tea ball or cheesecloth
- 8 cups (2 L) water (for cooking beans)
- 1 Tbsp salt

For Finishing the Beans:
- ¼ cup (60 ml) olive oil
- 1 bell pepper, diced
- ½ large onion, diced
- 3 garlic cloves, minced
- ¼ cup (60 ml) white wine
- 1 tsp white vinegar
- 1 tsp sugar
- ½ tsp cumin
- ½ tsp dried oregano
- Salt to taste

1. Pick through and rinse the black beans, then put them in a large bowl and cover by 2–3 inches (5–7.5 cm) with cold water. Set aside to soak overnight (the beans will increase in volume 2–3 times while they soak, depending on how old they are).

2. The following day, drain and rinse the beans. Heat the olive oil in a large pot or pressure cooker and sauté the onion and garlic until soft. Add the beans, culantro, and 8 cups (2 L) water to the pot. Bring to a boil, reduce heat, and simmer, covered, until beans are tender, 40–60 mins. (If using a pressure cooker, lock pressure cooker and bring up to pressure at medium-high heat. When you start to hear a hissing sound, reduce the heat and cook for 20–25 mins. Remove from heat and let the pressure out naturally by setting aside for 15–20 mins.) During this time the beans will begin to thicken, and the diced onion and garlic will practically melt into the beans. Once the beans are soft, add 1 Tbsp salt and remove the culantro.

3. To finish the beans, first make the sofrito: Heat the olive oil in a skillet and sauté the pepper, onions, and garlic until cooked but still a little firm. Fold the sofrito into the beans then add the white wine, vinegar, sugar, cumin, and oregano. Remove from the heat and salt to taste.

Sopa de Frijoles: Black Bean Soup
Make the recipe for Potaje de Frijoles Negros. Scoop out 3 cups (510 g) cooked beans and blend until smooth (or use an immersion blender), then stir back into the pot. This offers a hearty textured soup. Garnish with minced cilantro.

Frijoles Dormidos: Sleeping Beans
Many Cuban home cooks share the opinion that beans taste best the next day. These make-ahead beans will have a stiffer consistency than the previous recipes. Make the recipe for Potaje de Frijoles Negros. Drain off 1–3 cups (240–700 g) of the cooking liquid (discard or reuse in another recipe). Let the beans cool, then cover and refrigerate overnight. The next day, warm the beans over low heat. Add 1 Tbsp white vinegar, 1 tsp sugar, and any dry spices desired, such as a pinch of cumin and oregano. Salt to taste.

Potaje de FRIJOLES COLORADOS

Stewed Red Beans • Serves 8

This is a hearty stew, rich in meat, starches & vegetables. To make a more basic red beans dish, known as moros (beans), omit the meat, plantains, carrots, and squash.

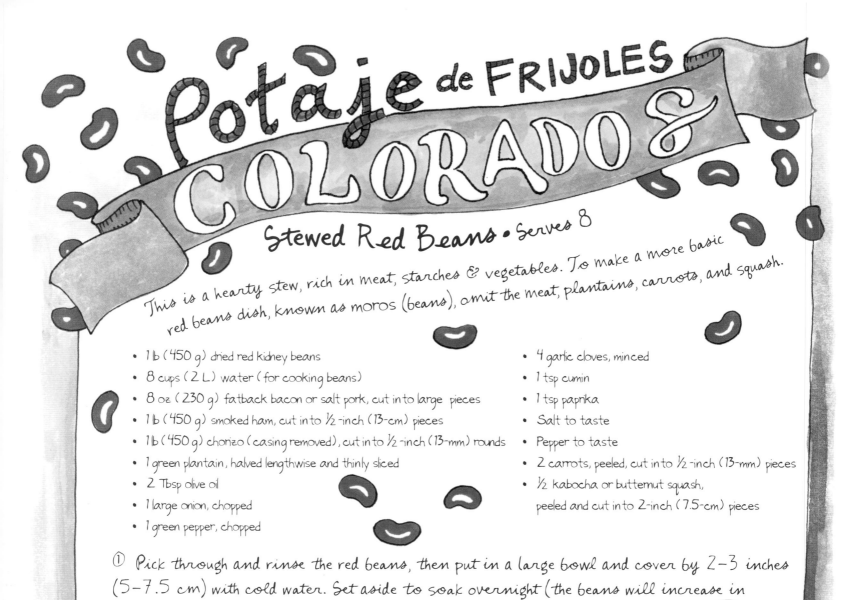

- 1 lb (450 g) dried red kidney beans
- 8 cups (2 L) water (for cooking beans)
- 8 oz (230 g) fatback bacon or salt pork, cut into large pieces
- 1 lb (450 g) smoked ham, cut into ½-inch (13-cm) pieces
- 1 lb (450 g) chorizo (casing removed), cut into ½-inch (13-mm) rounds
- 1 green plantain, halved lengthwise and thinly sliced
- 2 Tbsp olive oil
- 1 large onion, chopped
- 1 green pepper, chopped

- 4 garlic cloves, minced
- 1 tsp cumin
- 1 tsp paprika
- Salt to taste
- Pepper to taste
- 2 carrots, peeled, cut into ½-inch (13-mm) pieces
- ½ kabocha or butternut squash, peeled and cut into 2-inch (7.5-cm) pieces

① Pick through and rinse the red beans, then put in a large bowl and cover by 2–3 inches (5–7.5 cm) with cold water. Set aside to soak overnight (the beans will increase in volume 2–3 times while they soak, depending on how old they are).

② The following day, drain and rinse the beans. Add 8 cups (2 L) water to a large pot with the beans and bring to a boil, cover, lower heat, and simmer until beans are tender, 1 hr. If using a pressure cooker, lock lid and bring up to pressure following manufacturer's directions and cook for 20–25 mins over high heat. Remove from heat and let the pressure out slowly by setting aside for 15–20 mins.

③ While beans are cooking, combine the bacon, ham, chorizo, sliced plantains, and olive oil in a heavy skillet over medium heat and cook until browned, about 5 mins. Add the onions, peppers, and garlic and cook until soft. Add cumin, paprika, salt, and pepper and sauté for 1 min more. Remove from the heat and set aside until beans are tender.

④ Once the beans are tender, add the carrots, squash, and meat-sofrito mixture to the beans and cook until everything is soft, about 30 mins. Serve with rice.

CONGRÍ

Rice & Beans • Serves 8

This dish is also known as *Moros y Cristianos* (Moors and Christians)—rice and beans sharing the same plate. This recipe can be made vegetarian, and is often prepared that way in Cuba. Simply omit the meat.

> 1 lb (450 g) cooked beans (*Potaje de Frijoles Negros*, page 52, prepared through step 2)
> 8 oz (230 g) thick-cut bacon, cut into 1-inch (2.5-cm) squares
> 1 lb (450 g) chorizo, cut into ½-inch (13-mm) rounds
> 1 medium onion, chopped
> 5 ají cachucha, stemmed and chopped, or 1 green bell pepper, chopped
> 2 garlic cloves, minced
> 2 cups (400 g) long-grain white rice
> 1 Tbsp salt
> 2 tsp cumin
> 4 culantro leaves or 1 cup (50 g) chopped cilantro
> ¼ cup (60 ml) fresh lime juice
> ¼ (60 ml) cup olive oil

1. Drain the cooked beans in a colander set over a bowl to catch the cooking liquid. Reserve 3 cups (700 ml) of the liquid, which will be black, for cooking the rice; set aside.

2. Sauté the bacon in a saucepan over medium heat, stirring occasionally, until crisp. Add the chorizo and sauté until lightly browned, about 4 mins. Drain off some of the fat, then add the chopped onions and peppers and continue to cook until onions are translucent, about 5 mins. Add the minced garlic and cook for 1 min.

3. Add the rice, salt, cumin, and culantro leaves and cook, stirring, until rice is lightly browned, about 5 mins. Stir in the reserved bean cooking liquid, bring to a boil, then reduce the heat and simmer, covered, until rice is tender, about 15 mins.

4. Once the rice is cooked, add 2–3 cups cooked beans (there will be some beans left over), stir together gently, and cook for 5 mins more. Remove from the heat and stir in the lime juice and olive oil.

Potaje de GARBANZOS

GARBANZO STEW • SERVES 6–8

I learned this dish from Lázaro, a professional chef and friend of a friend with whom I cooked several times during my stay in central Havana. Lázaro always brought his own spices, things I couldn't find at the agromercado (outdoor market), including three different kinds of fresh oregano that he grew in his garden. If you're cooking the beans on the stovetop, soak the beans overnight to reduce their cooking time.

- 1 lb (450 g) garbanzo beans (soaked overnight, drained)
- 8 cups (2 L) water
- 4 fresh orégano cubano leaves (page 152) or substitute for 2 Tbsp small-leaf variety of oregano
- 1 Tbsp olive oil
- 1 lb (450 g) chorizo, casing removed, cut into ½-inch (13-mm) rounds
- 1 large onion, chopped

- 1 green bell pepper, sliced
- 4 garlic cloves, minced
- 1 tsp cumin
- 1 tsp paprika
- 1 tsp freshly ground pepper
- Salt to taste
- 2 carrots, cut into ½-inch (13-mm) rounds
- Pinch of sugar

1. Combine the garbanzo beans, water, and oregano leaves in a large pot or pressure cooker. Bring to a boil, cover, lower heat, and simmer until beans are tender. This will take about 1 hour on the stovetop or 10–15 mins in a pressure cooker over high heat, once pressure is reached with quick pressure release (follow manufacturer's directions).

2. Meanwhile, make the sofrito: Heat olive oil in a large skillet and sauté the chorizo, onions, peppers, and garlic until soft. Add cumin, paprika, pepper, and salt to taste and sauté for 1 min. Remove from the heat and set aside.

3. Once beans are tender, stir in the carrots and sofrito and cook for an additional 30 mins on stovetop, or 5–7 mins in pressure cooker, once pressure is reached. Add salt and a pinch of sugar to taste. Serve with white rice.

POTAJE de CHÍCHAROS

SPLIT PEA STEW
Serves 6

Chícharos have long been a common component in the monthly Cuban food rations, and although this is a well-liked dish, it reminds many people of a time when all they had to eat were dried split peas, during the Special Period (see page 77). If you have it, it's nice to reuse the cooking liquid from making Ropa Vieja (page 34) in place of beef stock here.

- 1 lb (450 g) green or yellow split peas
- 1 lb (450 g) smoked ham shank
- 6 cups (14 dL) beef stock
- 2 Tbsp olive oil
- 1 large onion, chopped
- 1 large green bell pepper, chopped
- 4 cloves minced garlic
- 2 tsp cumin
- 4–6 culantro leaves or ½ cup (25 g) chopped cilantro
- Salt
- 1 lb (450 g) chorizo, casing removed, cut into 1-inch (2.5-cm) pieces
- 4 potatoes, peeled and cut into 1-inch (2.5-cm) pieces
- 2 carrots, cut into ½-inch (13-mm) pieces
- ½ kabocha squash, peeled and cut into 2-inch (5-cm) pieces

1. In a large soup pot, combine the split peas, ham shank, and stock and bring to a boil. Cover, lower heat, and simmer.

2. While the peas are simmering, make the sofrito: Heat the olive oil in a skillet over medium-high heat and sauté onions, peppers, and garlic. Add cumin, culantro leaves, and salt to taste, then add the chorizo and cook until browned.

3. Add the sofrito to the simmering peas and cook until the peas begin to soften, about 20 mins. Add the potatoes and carrots and cook for about 10 mins. Lower the heat and stir frequently to prevent the soup from sticking. Add the squash and cook until all the vegetables are tender, about 10 mins more. If you like, shred the meat from the ham shank and stir into the soup.

Ensalada de Frijoles Blancos

White Bean Salad

Make this salad with navy or cannellini beans or black-eyed peas, known as *frijoles de carita* (beans with little faces).

Serves 6–8

Salad:
1 lb (450 g) dried white beans
1 Tbsp salt
8 oz (230 g) small potatoes
1 medium onion, thinly sliced
¼ cup (25 g) coarsely chopped green olives
¼ cup (36 g) chopped parsley

Aliño (Dressing):
1 garlic clove, finely minced
½ cup (120 ml) olive oil
¼ cup (60 ml) white vinegar
Salt to taste

Optional: Place the beans in a bowl, cover with plenty of water, and let soak overnight. Drain and rinse.

Conventional cooking method: Place beans and salt in a pot, cover with fresh water, bring to a boil, and then lower to a simmer. Presoaked beans should be tender after 1 hr; unsoaked beans may take 2 hrs to become tender. Add the potatoes and more water if needed to cover, and cook over low heat for another 30–40 mins until the beans are tender, but still intact, and the potatoes are soft. Drain and let cool.

Pressure cooker method: Rinse dry, unsoaked beans, place in pressure cooker with salt, and add 8 cups (2 L) water. Lock lid, bring up to pressure, and cook for 15 mins. Release pressure, add potatoes, and bring up to pressure. Cook for another 5 mins, then release pressure, drain, and cool.

To make the *aliño* (dressing), stir together garlic, oil, vinegar, and salt to taste. When the potatoes and beans are cool, peel the potatoes and cut into bite-size cubes. Place the potatoes and beans in a mixing bowl, along with the onions, olives, and parsley. Pour the *aliño* over the salad and gently mix to combine. Cover and chill until ready to serve.

Tamal en Cazuela

Deconstructed Tamale • Serves 8

This dish embodies what is a classic Cuban *plato fuerte* (main course): a one-pot meal cooked in a *cazuela* (a large heavy pot, like a Dutch oven), in which pork, vegetables, starch, and carbs all simmer together, offering up a satisfying meal. When avocados are in season, they make a delicious and eye-catching finishing touch to each serving.

For Cooking:

- ¼ cup (60 ml) olive oil, plus 1 Tbsp
- 1 onion, chopped
- 1 green bell pepper, cored and chopped
- 2 garlic cloves, minced
- 1 tsp cumin
- 1 cup (240 ml) *vino seco* or dry white wine
- ½ cup (120 ml) tomato sauce
- 2 cups (350 g) frozen corn
- 2 Tbsp water
- 3 cups (700 ml) chicken stock
- 1½ cups (207 g) fine cornmeal
- Juice of 1 lime
- ½ tsp achiote oil (optional)
- Salt and pepper to taste
- 2 scallions, chopped
- ½ cup (25 g) cilantro leaves

For Pork:

- 1½ lb (675 g) pork shoulder, cut into ½-inch (13-mm) cubes
- 1 garlic clove, minced
- 1 tsp salt
- ½ tsp cumin
- ½ tsp freshly ground pepper

❶ Combine the pork, garlic, salt, cumin, and pepper in a bowl and toss together until the pork is seasoned all over. Cover tightly and marinate, refrigerated, for at least 3 hrs or overnight.

❷ Heat ¼ cup (60 ml) olive oil in a large skillet over medium-high heat and brown the pork. Add the onion and bell pepper and cook until softened; then stir in the garlic and cumin and cook for 1 min more. Stir in the wine and tomato sauce, cover and reduce the heat. Simmer for about 30 mins, allowing flavors to meld.

❸ Meanwhile, combine the frozen corn with 2 Tbsp water and remaining 1 Tbsp olive oil in a food processor and pulse until coarsely ground. Scrape the corn into a large pot; whisk in the stock and cornmeal. Cook over medium heat, stirring frequently, until thickened, 5–10 mins. Add ¾ of the cooked pork (reserve the rest to add on top), the lime juice, and the achiote oil, and continue to cook for about 30 mins. Season to taste with salt and pepper. Serve with some of the remaining pork on top and garnish with scallions and cilantro.

❹ Serve with avocado slices and *Plátanos Fritos* (page 80).

TAMALES de MAÍZ

Field Corn Tamales • Makes 18–24

In Cuba, most of the corn grown is field or dent corn, which is starchier and has a much larger kernel than the sweet corn to which North Americans are accustomed. Although it is edible, field corn is mostly grown as animal feed in the US. If you know a farmer who grows this variety, get it fresh and prepare tamales just as they do in Cuba! A variation using our common sweet corn is also included below. You can omit the pork to make them vegetarian; this will reduce the yield.

> 2½ – 3 lbs (1.1–1.4 kg) fresh dent or field corn ears (about 10 ears) with husks
> 1 lb (450 g) pork shoulder, minced (if there's fat to trim, render and use instead of olive oil)
> ¼ cup (60 ml) olive oil or rendered pork fat
> 1 red bell pepper, minced
> 1 onion, minced
> 2 garlic cloves, mashed
> 1 cup (240 ml) tomato sauce or 4 oz (120 ml) tomato paste mixed with 4 oz (120 ml) water
> 1 Tbsp cumin
> 1 Tbsp sugar
> Salt and pepper

With the leaves on, cut ¼ inch (6 mm) from base and top of ears of corn, then roll off leaves, keeping whole. These will be used as the tamale wrappers and *lazos* (ties).

To make the *lazos*, tear a corn leaf lengthwise into a 1-inch (2.5-cm) strip. Tie an overhand knot at the top end of the leaf, then tear the leaf lengthwise again to make the piece twice as long (the knot will be in the middle of the *lazo*). Make 25–30 ties.

Cut corn kernels from the cobs and place in a food processor. Pulse until the kernels are coarsely chopped. Transfer the corn mixture to a colander set over a bowl and let sit until the excess starchy water has drained off; discard liquid.

Heat the oil or rendered fat in a skillet over medium-high heat and sauté the pork for 2 mins. Add red pepper, onion, and garlic and cook until soft. Add tomato sauce and cumin and simmer for 15 mins. Add sugar and salt and pepper to taste; continue cooking for 10–15 mins. Stir the drained corn into the meat mixture and cook until it thickens, about 20 mins. Cool.

⑤ To assemble the tamales, arrange 2 cornhusks on a large surface and overlap them. Drop 2 heaping Tbsp of the corn mixture in the center of the husks. Fold the husks, first the short way, then long way, making a little package. Tie with 1 or 2 of the corn leaf *lassos* in the center of the tamale to secure it.

⑥ Arrange the tamales in a large steamer pot, standing them on end, and cover. Bring the water to a boil. Reduce heat and steam, covered, for 1–1½ hrs. Tamales can be made ahead and kept refrigerated or frozen.

VARIATION: Tamales con maíz dulce y masa
Tamales with Sweet Corn and Masa

If preparing with fresh corn, keep the husks to use as wrappers. If making with frozen corn, purchase a package of dried cornhusks, available at Latin markets and many grocery stores.

Follow directions, replacing the field corn with 3 cups (525 g) fresh or frozen sweet corn. After all other ingredients are added to the pan, including the corn, add 1 cup (113 g) masa harina and 1 cup (240 ml) chicken broth, a little at a time, and cook until mixture thickens, about 20 mins. Let sit until cool. Continue with directions above for assembling tamales. Makes about 20 tamales.

DEL MAR

From the Sea

Buscando Mariscos

Searching for Seafood

Pedro Duperey has spent most of his life in Havana. Outgoing, friendly, and proud, he knows most everyone on the streets in the area. Pedro was just the type of person I needed to help track down fresh seafood in a city where one seldom finds it for sale in the outdoor markets. We asked around, got our first recommendation, and were hot on the trail.

Calling up at balconies, "*Buscamos a Manuel—¿si tiene pescado?*" ("We're looking for Manuel—does he have fish?") "*Ya, no . . . Vaya a ver a Celia en la casa morada.*" ("Not anymore . . . go see Celia in the purple house.") We reached Celia's home two blocks south and climbed the narrow staircase, knocked, and waited . . . "*Se fue, alía para la tarde,*" she exclaimed. ("He's gone, out for the afternoon.") I made sure to jot down his phone number for future reference.

We went to six different homes in *La Habana Vieja* (Old Havana), based on word of mouth, searching for a fresh catch. It was late in the day and three of the potential sources had already sold out. We stopped at the ration distribution center, and the man on duty recommended we check next door. "*No es un pescador, pero teine un congelador.*" ("He's not a fisherman, but he has a freezer.") We knocked, and two kids answered the door. We explained what we were there for, and they led us through an easement between the homes into a garden patio area, where we waited. A man appeared and showed us into his living room, where a large freezer chest stood in the small space. There it was—an 8-lb (3.6 kg) sierra (a fish related to the tuna), frozen. Pedro and I scanned the fish and agreed it would do. I paid 15 Cuban pesos (CUCs) for it, about half the amount many Cubans make in a month, and we headed home to cook.

It was this experience that contributed to my understanding of seafood in Cuba, at least at this moment in time in Havana: Simply put, fish, octopus and shellfish are hard to come by. The exact cause for this is complex. One contributing factor may be the limited number of commercial fishing licenses off of Havana Bay. Another reason is that much of the day's catch is reserved for export or bought in volume by the restaurant industry, a business that is booming as a result of the growing popularity of *paladares* (private restaurants). Any small quantity of the leftover catch is often frozen and sold by word of mouth in the streets, as I experienced with Pedro.

When I traveled to the small towns of the east coast, seafood was more readily available to locals (not just the restaurant trade). This may be because that part of the island is less densely populated and the surrounding waters are richer in seafood of all types. In my experience, the day's catch is bought from the fisherman at the water's edge or from a street vendor selling from a small cart. In the coastal towns of Baracoa, Gibara, and Trinidad, I ate my fair share of shrimp, fish, lobster, and even shark with the locals, and obtaining seafood didn't require an extensive network of connections. Without a complex food distribution system within the country, Cubans really do eat what is produced locally and regionally, reflected by the distinctive cuisines from one end of the island to the other.

Cóctel de Ostiones & Camarones

Oyster and Shrimp Cocktail • Serves 4

On many streets in Cuba there are little metal carts that sell all kinds of things, from shaved ice to sandwiches. In the little town of Gibara on the northeast coast, you'll find many carts along the coastline selling *cóctel de ostiones y camarones*. The concept is simple—superfresh seafood served in a glass to be shot back with lime, tomato juice, and a splash of hot sauce. Enjoy with a cold Cristal or Bucanero, the two most common beers in Cuba, which are produced just 45 minutes away in the city of Holguín.

offertas:
camarón...5¢
ostiones...6¢

▷ 12 fresh oysters or freshly steamed small or medium-sized shrimp, peeled
▷ 3 cups (700 ml) tomato juice
▷ 2 limes
▷ Salt
▷ Ground black pepper
▷ Tabasco or your favorite cayenne hot sauce, optional

Using an oyster knife, carefully shuck the oysters and/or shrimp. Drop 3-4 into each tumbler glass. Stir in tomato juice, a squeeze of lime, a pinch of salt and pepper, and Tabasco, if you like. Serve at once.

64

CAMARONES CRIOLLOS
• Shrimp Creole •

Use this savory shrimp recipe as a filling for tostones or even empanadas. It can also be served over rice for a satisfying, easy main dish.

Serves 4–6 over rice, or fills about 20 tostones or 15 empanadas

¼ cup (60 ml) olive oil
½ onion, finely diced
½ red bell pepper, finely diced
2 garlic cloves, minced
1½ lb (675 g) raw shrimp, peeled, cleaned, and coarsely chopped
¼ cup (15 g) chopped cilantro
1 tsp paprika
1 tsp salt
½ tsp cumin

Heat olive oil in a skillet over medium heat and sauté onions and peppers until soft and slightly golden. Add garlic and sauté 1 min more.

Add shrimp, cilantro, paprika, salt, and cumin and sauté until shrimp is just cooked through, 3–4 mins.

Remove from the heat and spoon into tostones or serve over rice.

Camarones Enchilados

Shrimp in Tomato & Pepper Sauce • Serves 4

The word *enchilados* refers to the sauce; in Cuba, this is a mild tomato-based mixture with bell peppers.

- ¼ cup (60 ml) olive oil
- 1 medium onion, diced
- 1 red bell pepper, diced
- 1 green bell pepper, diced
- ¼ cup (23 g) chopped ají cachucha
- 3 garlic cloves, minced
- 1 tsp paprika, divided
- 1 tsp cumin
- 1 tsp salt, divided
- ½ tsp pepper
- 4 plum tomatoes, seeded and chopped
- ½ cup (25 g) chopped cilantro, divided
- ¼ cup (60 ml) vino seco (dry white wine)
- 1 lb (450 g) large raw shrimp, peeled and deveined
- 4 Tbsp (57 g) butter
- Garnish: lime wedges, cilantro, and sliced avocado

Heat olive oil in a large skillet over medium heat and sauté onion and peppers until soft. Add garlic and sauté for 1 min, then add ½ tsp paprika, cumin, 1 tsp salt and pepper and cook for 1 min or so. Add tomatoes and half the cilantro and continue to cook, 2 more mins. Reduce heat, add vino seco, and simmer for 15—20 mins.

In a small bowl, stir together remaining ½ tsp paprika and ½ tsp salt; sprinkle over shrimp.

Heat butter in a large skillet over medium-high heat. Add shrimp and cook about 1 min per side. Stir in the sauce and cook for another minute—until shrimp are tender, but not overcooked.

Serve over white rice or *Harina de Maíz*, (page 45). Garnish with lime wedges, the remaining cilantro, and avocado slices.

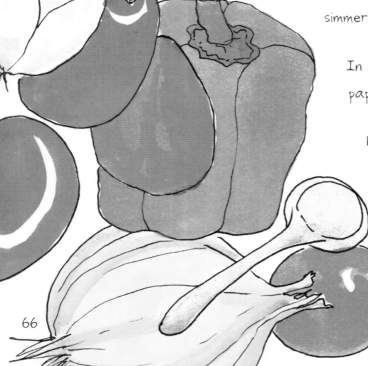

JAIBAS RELLENAS

Stuffed Blue Crab Shells • Serves 6-8

This meal is typical of Gibara and I really like the presentation—it's a fun party dish. Although they are similar in size, these blue crabs should not be confused with the land crabs of Cuba. The latter species of crab migrates every spring, traveling across wooded areas to the coastline to hatch their eggs, flooding the roads and even covering the walls of buildings! Though they are quite a sight, land crabs contain a harmful toxin and are not to be eaten by humans, but are a hearty meal for some mammals and birds.

- ¼ cup (60 ml) vegetable oil
- 1 green bell pepper, diced
- 1 red bell pepper, diced
- 1 onion, diced
- 3 garlic cloves, minced
- 1 cup (200 g) tomatoes, diced (canned okay)
- 2 Tbsp white vinegar
- 2 Tbsp vino seco (dry white wine)

- ½ teaspoon pimentón (smoked paprika)
- Salt and pepper
- 8 cooked blue crabs, crabmeat picked out and drained, shells saved for presentation (yields ½ lb (230 g) fresh lump crabmeat)
- ½ cup (56 g) dry bread crumbs
- ¼ cup (60 ml) lime juice
- Tabasco or other cayenne-based hot sauce

Heat oil in a large pan over medium heat; add bell peppers, onion, and garlic and sauté until translucent. Add tomatoes, vinegar, vino seco, pimentón, ½ tsp salt, and ¼ tsp pepper, and stir until warmed through, about 5 mins. Remove from heat. Fold in the crabmeat, bread crumbs, and lime juice. Adjust salt if necessary. Use a spoon to stuff the crab shells with the mixture. Serve with hot sauce on the side.

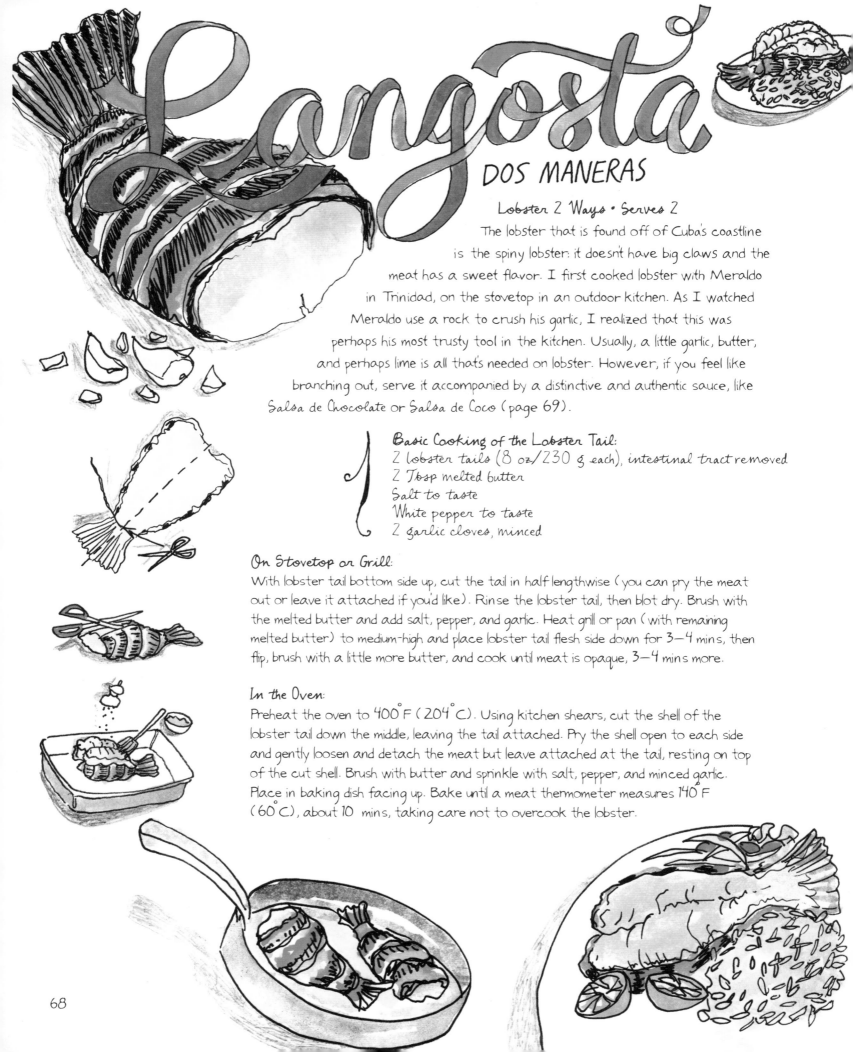

Langosta

DOS MANERAS

Lobster 2 Ways • Serves 2

The lobster that is found off of Cuba's coastline is the spiny lobster: it doesn't have big claws and the meat has a sweet flavor. I first cooked lobster with Meraldo in Trinidad, on the stovetop in an outdoor kitchen. As I watched Meraldo use a rock to crush his garlic, I realized that this was perhaps his most trusty tool in the kitchen. Usually, a little garlic, butter, and perhaps lime is all that's needed on lobster. However, if you feel like branching out, serve it accompanied by a distinctive and authentic sauce, like Salsa de Chocolate or Salsa de Coco (page 69).

Basic Cooking of the Lobster Tail:

2 lobster tails (8 oz/230 g each), intestinal tract removed
2 Tbsp melted butter
Salt to taste
White pepper to taste
2 garlic cloves, minced

On Stovetop or Grill:

With lobster tail bottom side up, cut the tail in half lengthwise (you can pry the meat out or leave it attached if you'd like). Rinse the lobster tail, then blot dry. Brush with the melted butter and add salt, pepper, and garlic. Heat grill or pan (with remaining melted butter) to medium-high and place lobster tail flesh side down for 3–4 mins, then flip, brush with a little more butter, and cook until meat is opaque, 3–4 mins more.

In the Oven:

Preheat the oven to 400°F (204°C). Using kitchen shears, cut the shell of the lobster tail down the middle, leaving the tail attached. Pry the shell open to each side and gently loosen and detach the meat but leave attached at the tail, resting on top of the cut shell. Brush with butter and sprinkle with salt, pepper, and minced garlic. Place in baking dish facing up. Bake until a meat thermometer measures 140°F (60°C), about 10 mins, taking care not to overcook the lobster.

CHEF SMITH:

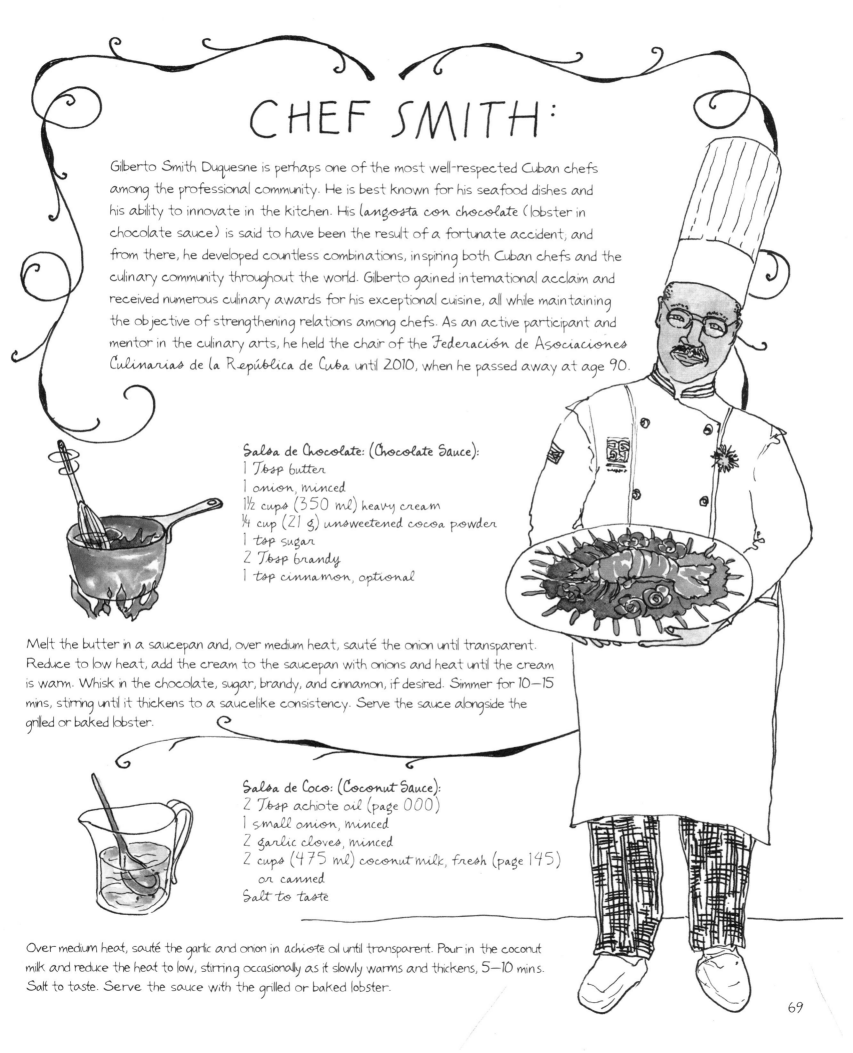

Gilberto Smith Duquesne is perhaps one of the most well-respected Cuban chefs among the professional community. He is best known for his seafood dishes and his ability to innovate in the kitchen. His *langosta con chocolate* (lobster in chocolate sauce) is said to have been the result of a fortunate accident, and from there, he developed countless combinations, inspiring both Cuban chefs and the culinary community throughout the world. Gilberto gained international acclaim and received numerous culinary awards for his exceptional cuisine, all while maintaining the objective of strengthening relations among chefs. As an active participant and mentor in the culinary arts, he held the chair of the *Federación de Asociaciones Culinarias de la República de Cuba* until 2010, when he passed away at age 90.

Salsa de Chocolate: (Chocolate Sauce):
1 Tbsp butter
1 onion, minced
1½ cups (350 ml) heavy cream
¼ cup (21 g) unsweetened cocoa powder
1 tsp sugar
2 Tbsp brandy
1 tsp cinnamon, optional

Melt the butter in a saucepan and, over medium heat, sauté the onion until transparent. Reduce to low heat, add the cream to the saucepan with onions and heat until the cream is warm. Whisk in the chocolate, sugar, brandy, and cinnamon, if desired. Simmer for 10–15 mins, stirring until it thickens to a saucelike consistency. Serve the sauce alongside the grilled or baked lobster.

Salsa de Coco: (Coconut Sauce):
2 Tbsp achiote oil (page 000)
1 small onion, minced
2 garlic cloves, minced
2 cups (475 ml) coconut milk, fresh (page 145)
  or canned
Salt to taste

Over medium heat, sauté the garlic and onion in achiote oil until transparent. Pour in the coconut milk and reduce the heat to low, stirring occasionally as it slowly warms and thickens, 5–10 mins. Salt to taste. Serve the sauce with the grilled or baked lobster.

Escabeche

Fish in Vinegar Pickle

de Pescado

Serves 6

Most vinegar-based recipes are founded on the idea that acid acts as a preservative, and *escabeche* is a perfect example of this approach. In Cuba, Emelio Companioni remembers his mother making *escabeche* in his hometown of Fomento and keeping it in a clay pot on an upper shelf in the kitchen. The fish, submerged in a vinegar marinade, kept for several days. *Escabeche* is different than ceviche in that the fish is fully cooked before the vinegar mixture is added.

The Pickle:

¾ cup (180 ml) olive oil
¾ cup (180 ml) white vinegar
6 garlic cloves, lightly crushed
1 (8-oz/230-g) jar alcaparrado (mix of green olives, capers, and pimentos) or 6 oz (173 g) green olives with pimentos, halved, and 2 Tbsp capers
2 bay leaves
1 tsp black peppercorns (keep these in a little pouch of cheesecloth or a tea ball)
1 tsp salt

The Fish:

2–3 lb (900–1,350 g) swordfish, kingfish, or mackerel, cut into 1-inch (2.5-cm) steaks
Salt and pepper
¼ cup (60 ml) olive oil
3 medium onions, sliced
2 bell peppers (1 green and 1 red), very thinly sliced (use a mandoline)

1 Rinse and pat fish dry. Season fish with salt and pepper.

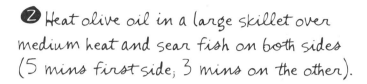

2 Heat olive oil in a large skillet over medium heat and sear fish on both sides (5 mins first side; 3 mins on the other).

3 Remove the fish from the pan and blot dry with paper towels to remove excess oil. Add the onions and peppers to the skillet and lightly fry until softened.

4 Combine all pickle ingredients in a large bowl, then fold in the peppers and onions.

5 In a clay pot or glass dish that has a cover, arrange alternate layers of the pickle mixture and fish, beginning and finishing with the pickle mixture. Fish can be on 1 layer or carefully stacked.

6 Cover and allow the dish to marinate at least 24 hrs in a cool place (escabeche technically does not need to be refrigerated, since the vinegar pickle preserves it). It can be kept for up to 3 days at room temperature, or a week in the refrigerator.

7 Before serving, discard bay leaves, break apart the fish in the dish, and serve at room temperature.

Sopa de Pescado
FISH SOUP

Serves 6-8

> 1-(3 lb/1.4 kg) red snapper
> 2 large onions, separated
> 3 garlic cloves, separated
> 2 bay leaves
> 8 cups (2 L) water
> 2 Tbsp olive oil
> 1 small red bell pepper, chopped
> 1 small green bell pepper, chopped

> 3 tomatoes, peeled, seeded, and chopped
> ¼ cup (25 g) chopped parsley
> 1 tsp cumin
> 1 tsp dried oregano
> 1 tsp sweet paprika
> Salt and pepper
> 4 potatoes, peeled and cut into ½-inch (13-mm) pieces
> 4 oz (113 g) fine noodles, such as angel hair, broken into 2-inch (5-cm) lengths
> Juice of 1 lime
> 1 lime, cut into wedges

Ask your fishmonger to clean, fillet, and skin a whole 3-lb (1.4-kg) snapper for you, but make sure to take all the trimmings (the head, skin, and bones) for making the stock (page 30).

Chop the fish into bite-size pieces and set aside. Place the trimmings in a stockpot. Quarter 1 of the onions and mash 2 of the garlic cloves; add to the pot along with the bay leaves and 8 cups (2 L) water. Bring to a boil, then reduce heat and simmer for 45 mins. Strain the stock through a fine-mesh sieve (you should have 6–7 cups/14–16 dL); set aside.

Chop the remaining onion and garlic clove. Heat the oil in a pot; add the onion, garlic, and bell peppers and cook until softened. Add the tomatoes, parsley, spices, salt, and pepper to taste and continue to cook for a few minutes more. Add the potatoes and fish stock and bring to a boil. Lower the heat and simmer for 10 mins. Add the noodles and fish and cook until noodles and potatoes are tender, 8–10 mins. Add the lime juice.

Serve the soup with the lime wedges and crusty bread on the side.

Cómo Cortar un Limón
How to Cut a Lime

1   2   3

Make the most of your lime! To yield as much juice as possible, cut the lime in 3 parts: Slice ⅓ off the side, then cut the larger, remaining piece in half.

Pargo al Horno

Serves 3–4

Chef Alberto Ronda teaches culinary classes in Gibara a few times a week, and I had the pleasure of joining him one day. Decked out in their chefs' coats, his enthusiastic class of 20 students buzzed about the kitchen and prepared a large baked snapper stuffed with vegetables along with sweet potato chips, battered shark fillets, stuffed crab shells, and rice and beans—all while cooking the daily lunch specials of the Casa del Chef, a restaurant run by the culinary school.

Ingredients:
- 1 whole snapper, 2.5–3 lb (1.1–1.4 kg)
- Salt
- 3 garlic cloves, minced
- Juice of 1 lime
- 2 tomatoes, diced
- 1 onion, diced
- 3 bell peppers
  (dice 2 peppers and slice the 3rd for garnish)
- Mojo Clásico (page 15), for serving

Baked Snapper

Clean and scale the whole snapper (or ask your fish seller to do this), then rinse it well and rub with salt, garlic, and lime juice, inside and out. Place the fish on a baking sheet lined with aluminum foil and stuff the cavity with the diced bell peppers, tomatoes, and onion. Let the fish sit, refrigerated, for at least 1 hour.

Preheat the oven to 350°F (177°C). Bake fish until the meat is opaque white and separates easily near the center of the fish, 30–40 mins. Transfer to a platter. Arrange the sliced peppers around the fish and serve with mojo sauce on the side.

VIANDAS, VEGETALES Y FRUTAS

Viandas • Starches

Vegetales • Vegetables

Frutas • Fruits

El Período Especial y Organopónicos
The Special Period and Cuba's Urban Farms

A quilt of organic, urban farms blankets Cuba. Its formation during the 1990s was prompted by necessity rather than choice—a tactical measure to increase food production during the Período Especial (the Special Period), the most significant economic depression in Cuba's modern history. In exchange for sugar, the country's single most important export commodity, Cuba had received most of its imports from the Soviet Union—from oil and food products to technology and medicine. When the USSR fell apart, beginning in 1989, the sudden lack of resources led to devastation for Cuba and its citizens. People were out of work and hungry (the average Cuban lost 20 lbs/9 kg), and meeting basic needs was a challenge.

Due to gasoline and diesel oil shortages, the country had to reimagine its transportation and agricultural systems, converting former sugarcane fields into fruit and vegetable crops. Because Cuba could no longer obtain agricultural pesticides, growing crops organically became a necessity. The government began to distribute sections of land surrounding urban centers to anyone willing to start small-scale farms. When I visited Organopónico Vivero Alamar, one of Havana's largest organic farms, production manager Gonzalo Gonzalez explained how the foundation of cooperitives has grown tremendously in the last 30 years. There are more than 160 urban farms around Havana and 2,000 total throughout the country, nearly all of them organic. This approach of growing varied produce close to consumers greatly reduces the cost of transportation, thus getting the products out more efficiently while using fewer resources. These farms have adapted organic growing techniques to optimize yields, using manure as the foundation for fertilizer and sprays made from fermented herbs to control pests.

Although Cuba now trades with countries throughout the world for a variety of goods, the inability to trade freely with its closest neighbor, the United States, has stifled its ability to make a significant recovery from the Special Period, and shortages persist even today. During my trips, I saw firsthand how hard it could be to find milk at the neighborhood supermarkets. The flour section of the grocery store could be bare for a few days, while an overwhelming quantity of vegetable oil sat nearby. People still shop with the mentality that if you see an item that you might need later, buy it now. It may not be there the next time you go to the supermarket.

Root Vegetables & Starches

Viandas are an essential part of any typical Cuban meal. These are root vegetables and starchy fruits—and there are a lot of them! Many of these viandas can be found fresh in the exotic produce section of the grocery store as well as in Latin American markets. They may have different names depending on which culture the store caters to; for example, malanga is called yautía in Puerto Rico, and sweet potato is known as camote in many Latin American countries. When preparing most viandas for cooking, submerge the peeled and chopped pieces in a bowl of water to avoid oxidation.

Malanga:

Closely related to the taro root, malanga is about the size and shape of a regular white potato with a brown, somewhat hairy skin. There are 4 different varieties: *blanco* (white), *amarillo* (yellow), *morada* (beige), or *isleña* (speckled brown). The cooked taste is nuttier than a sweet potato, and when boiled, the lighter ones may darken slightly.

Mapuey:

With its brown, rough skin and white flesh, this yam has a flavor and appearance similar to malanga but is rounder in shape.

Ñame:

Also known as tropical or African yam, this African sweet potato has a rough, dark brown skin with white, yellow, or pink flesh. It is prepared and eaten like malanga.

Boniato:

Translated, its name means "sweet and harmless." This starchy tuber has a chestnutlike flavor and a fluffy consistency and is less sweet and moist than other tubers. It is often referred to as the "Cuban sweet potato."

Plátanos:

Plantains are used in Cuban dishes at all stages of maturity—verde (green), pintón (semiripe), and maduro (ripe to the point of blackness).

- Plátano fruta or plátano manzano: a banana, eat raw.
- Plátano burro: eat mature, stewed in sugar as dessert.
- Plátano mancho: use for tostones, chicharitas (mariquitas).

Yuca:

The white flesh of the yuca is poisonous unless cooked. The older the root, the more fibrous its texture.

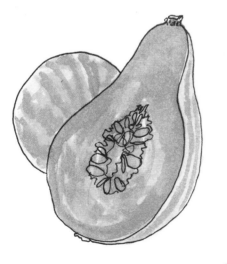

Calabaza:

Also called the West Indian pumpkin, this squash is oblong, with a broad body and narrower "neck." Its orange flesh has a sweet flavor and firm texture similar to butternut or kabocha squash.

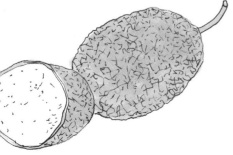

Guapén:

Also known as the bread fruit, the guapén has a really similar texture to a potato and malanga, but grows in a tall, large-leafed tree in Eastern Cuba. Also known as the Malanga del Árbol (Malanga Tree).

These sweet, fried plantains accompany many Cuban dishes. You must use very ripe plantains for this dish—look for ones that are soft with skins that are almost black or yellow with lots of black spots.

Plátanos Fritos

FRIED SWEET PLANTAINS • SERVES 4

3 large, very ripe plantains • Vegetable oil for frying

① Peel the plantains and cut them diagonally into 1-inch (2.5-cm) thick slices.

② Pour enough oil into a heavy 12-inch (30-cm) skillet to measure about ¼ inch (6 mm). Heat to 375°F (191°C), or you'll know the oil is hot enough if it sizzles when you flick a little water into the pan.

③ Fry the plantains, about 2 mins per side, then reduce the heat to low and continue to cook until the plantains are nicely caramelized. Use a slotted spoon to transfer to serving platter.

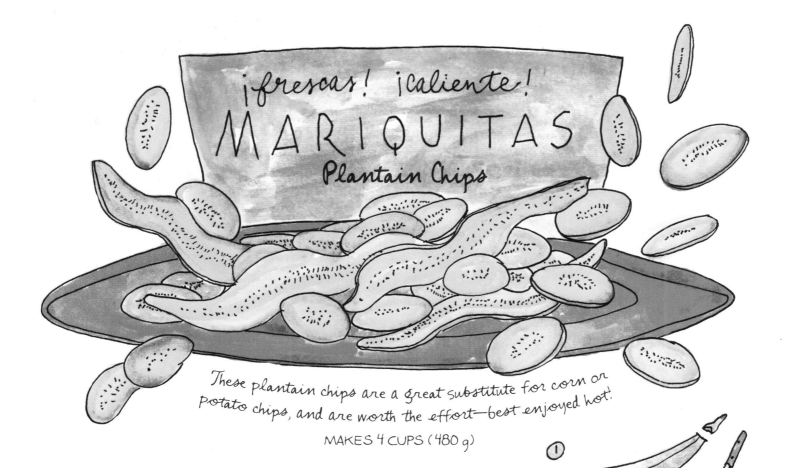

¡frescas! ¡caliente!
MARIQUITAS
Plantain Chips

These plantain chips are a great substitute for corn or potato chips, and are worth the effort—best enjoyed hot!

MAKES 4 CUPS (480 g)

4 GREEN PLANTAINS • VEGETABLE OIL FOR FRYING • SALT

▷ Bring a pot of water to a boil. Cut off the ends of the plantains and score the skin lengthwise along their natural ridges.

▷ Boil the plantains for 1–2 mins. Drain and run under cold water.

▷ When cool enough to handle, peel the plantains and slice into thin rounds.

▷ Heat 1 inch (2.5 cm) of oil in a heavy skillet (preferably cast-iron) to 370°F (188°C). In batches, fry the plantains until golden, flipping halfway through, about 5 mins. Keep an eye on them so they don't burn; frying happens quickly!

▷ Using a slotted spoon, transfer the fried plantains to a paper towel–lined plate to drain.

▷ Season with salt and serve immediately.

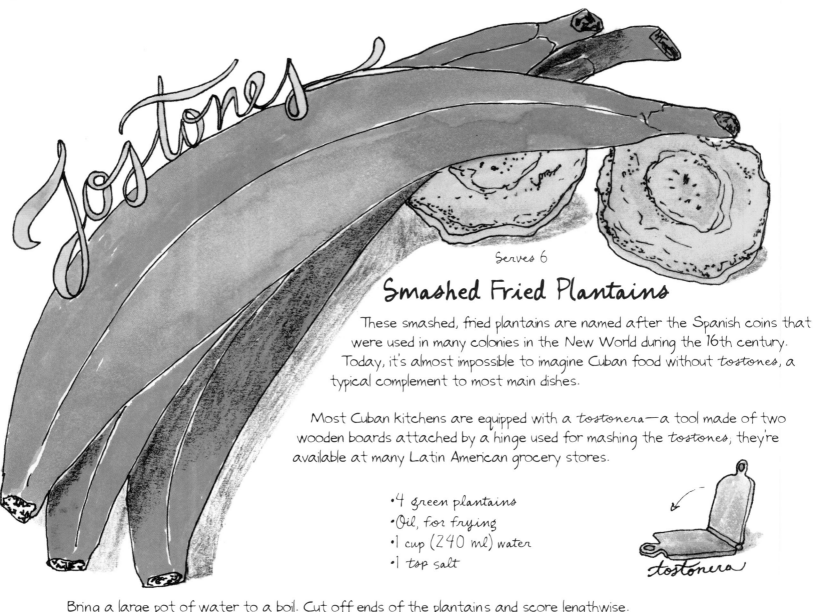

Serves 6

Smashed Fried Plantains

These smashed, fried plantains are named after the Spanish coins that were used in many colonies in the New World during the 16th century. Today, it's almost impossible to imagine Cuban food without *tostones*, a typical complement to most main dishes.

Most Cuban kitchens are equipped with a *tostonera*—a tool made of two wooden boards attached by a hinge used for mashing the *tostones*; they're available at many Latin American grocery stores.

- 4 green plantains
- Oil, for frying
- 1 cup (240 ml) water
- 1 tsp salt

tostonera

Bring a large pot of water to a boil. Cut off ends of the plantains and score lengthwise.

Follow steps 1 and 2 for making Tostones Rellenos, on opposite page.

After the first fry, let *tostones* cool for 5 mins, then gently smash each *tostón* using a *tostonera*. Alternatively, use a cup with a wide base to press each *tostón* so that it is about ¼-inch (6-mm) thick. Fry as directed in step 4 of opposite page. Lightly salt and serve. *Tostones* always taste best hot!

TOSTONES RELLENOS

Stuffed Plantain Cups
Serves 6

These cute little one-bite bowls filled with savory goodness are one of my favorite appetizers. I've included two types of fillings: *Camarones Criollos* (Shrimp Creole) and the classic *Picadillo* (Spiced Ground Beef). Note: You will need a *tostón* maker to form small 2-inch (5-cm) diameter cups. If you don't have one, a handheld citrus press makes a great alternative.

- 4 green plantains
- Oil, for frying
- 1 cup (240 ml) water
- 1 tsp salt

- Shrimp Creole (page 65) or Picadillo (page 38), for filling
- 2 scallions, finely chopped, for garnish

To Remove the Peel of Green Plantains More Easily:

Bring a large pot of water to a boil. Cut off ends of the plantains and score lengthwise through the skin along their natural ridges. Add the plantains to the water and boil for 1—2 mins (they will turn a darker, dull green). Drain and run the plantains under cold water until cool enough to handle. Peel and cut plantains crosswise into 1½-inch (4-cm) thick pieces.

First Fry:

Start heating oil in a deep pan over medium-high heat and add the plantains as the oil is heating. Fry the plantains, turning as necessary, until light golden on all sides. Transfer the pieces to a paper towel—lined plate to drain. Reserve the frying oil.

Shape the Tostones:

Place the freshly fried plantains, 1 at a time, in the center of the *tostón* maker and press into a bowl shape. Set aside on a plate.

Second Fry:

Heat the oil to 370°F (188°C). While oil is heating, mix the water and salt in a bowl. Working 1 at a time, quickly dip each *tostón* in the salted water, pat dry, then use tongs to place it carefully in the hot oil, taking care not to overcrowd the pan. Fry the *tostones* until they are golden brown, 1—3 mins. Place them on a fresh paper towel—lined plate to drain. Fill each *tostón* with a spoonful of the desired filling, garnish with scallions, and serve immediately.

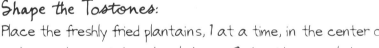

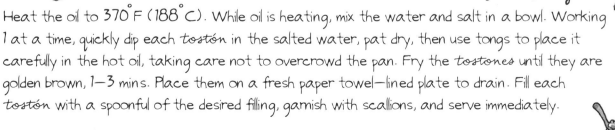

Bacán

Plantain Mash in Steamed Banana Leaves • Serves 8

Chef Antonio Solo roasts his pork on a spit, and with the leftovers he sometimes prepares bacán—a delicious mixture of plantains and meat steamed in a banana leaf. Antonio and fellow chef Yoeluis Binimelias prepared this very regional specialty for me one afternoon, and it was an immediate highlight of my trip. Bacán is similar to a tamale but made of plantain instead of corn—it's sweet, moist, and very flavorful. People will eat bacán with coffee for breakfast or as a snack at any point throughout the day.

Ingredients:

- 6 green plantains
- 3–4 garlic cloves
- 1 tsp salt
- ¼ tsp pepper
- ¼ cup (60 ml) sour orange juice
- 1 egg, beaten
- ¼ cup (60 ml) vegetable oil
- 1 cup (125 g) minced leftover roast pork or cooked crabmeat
- 1 tsp finely minced fresh oregano
- 4–8 pieces of banana leaf (8x8-inch/20x20-cm)
- Kitchen string

① Bring 2 quarts (2 L) water to a boil. Blanch the green plantains for 2–3 mins (this makes them easier to peel, but the plantains should still be firm). Let cool, then peel the plantains and submerge in a bowl of salted water as you work, to keep them from oxidizing. Grate enough plantain to measure about 3 cups.

② Mash together the garlic, salt, and pepper to make a paste. In a separate bowl, combine the garlic paste, sour orange juice, and egg. Pour the mixture over the grated plantain, add the oil, pork, and oregano, and stir well.

③ Drop 2 heaping Tbsp of the mixture onto the center of each banana leaf. Wrap up like a tamale, folding opposite sides toward each other to seal and tie with string.

④ Bring 6 cups (14 dL) water to a boil in a large steamer pot, arrange the packets in the steamer basket, cover, and simmer over medium heat about 45 mins, until the packet feels firm. Add more water if necessary to ensure the pot always has water in the bottom. Serve the bacán with cayenne hot sauce if you like.

Quimbombó con Plátano
A la Sefardí
Sephardic Okra with Plantains • Serves 4-6

- 1½ lb (775 g) okra
- 2 limes
- 2 Tbsp vegetable oil
- 1 onion, diced
- 3 cloves garlic, sliced

- 1 sweet ají cachucha pepper, diced (or ¼ green pepper, diced)
- ½ cup (120 ml) tomato sauce
- 1 Tbsp vino seco (dry white wine)
- 3 very ripe plantains, peeled

- ¼ tsp salt, plus more to taste
- 2 cups (475 ml) vegetable or chicken broth
- Cooked rice (for serving)

1. Slice the okra into about ½-inch (13-mm) thick rounds. Combine the lime juice with 8 cups of hot water in a large bowl. Add the sliced okra and soak for at least 10 mins, then rinse. (The acid from the limes helps reduce the okra's viscous texture.)

2. Heat vegetable oil in a Dutch oven or heavy pot, and make the sofrito. Cook onion, garlic, and ají cachucha pepper until soft. Mix in tomato sauce and wine. Bring to a simmer over medium-low heat for 5-10 mins, then remove from heat and set aside.

3. Heat the plantains in the microwave for 2-3 mins or cook in boiling water for 4-5 mins to soften. Cool.

4. Mash the plantains with ¼ tsp salt. With your hands, make about 30 balls, each 1 inch (2.5 cm) in diameter.

5. Return the Dutch oven to the stove. Add the broth and drained okra to the sofrito; simmer over medium heat until okra is tender, about 10 mins, salt to taste.

6. Add the plantain balls to the pot and simmer for another 10 mins. Serve with white rice.

This recipe is based on a dish I learned from Samy Sapayo, a Sephardic Jew born to Turkish parents in Cuba. Samy, a chef and entrepreneur, owned and operated an ice cream company located in Santiago de Cuba. After the revolution his business, like many others, was nationalized in 1961. At that point, Samy left Cuba for the United States. Samy's recipe is a great example of the fusion present in Cuban cooking: okra and plantains, both native to Africa, mingle with flavors of Spain and Turkey, along with the cachucha pepper, native to Cuba. Note: This can be a vegan dish.

Ensalada de Calabaza
Squash Salad

Serves 4–6

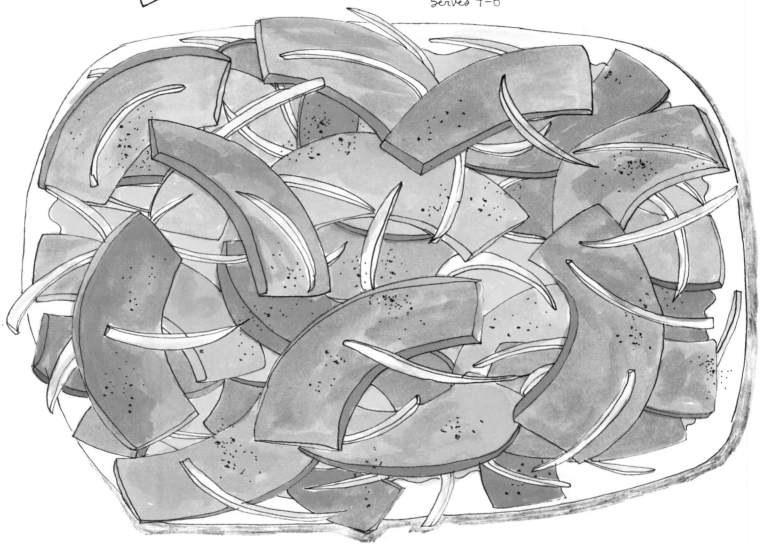

2 lb (900 g) calabaza (thin-skinned, orange-fleshed squash, such as kobocha or butternut)
Salt
½ cup (120 ml) olive oil
¼ cup (60 ml) vinegar

½ tsp dry mustard
2 large onions, thinly sliced
Lettuce leaves, for serving

1. Cut the squash into quarters, leaving the skin on. In a cazuela (large pot), add 3 inches (7.5 cm) of water and 1 Tbsp salt.
2. Add squash and cook*, covered, until flesh is tender and easily pierced with a fork but not mushy, 15—20 mins. Drain well and cool. (Note: Many cooks would save the cooking water, which is rich in nutrients, for making soup.)
3. As the squash is cooling, prepare the aliño (dressing). In a bowl, whisk together the oil, vinegar, mustard, and salt to taste. Add the onions and marinate for 10 mins.

4. When squash is cool enough to handle, peel and cut it into bite-size slices. Pour aliño and onions over squash and refrigerate.
5. Just before serving, arrange the lettuce leaves on a plate and spoon the cold salad over the greens.

*Alternatively, you can use a pressure cooker: Arrange squash pieces on cooking rack, lock lid, and bring to full pressure. Cook for 8 mins according to manufacturer's instructions, then reduce pressure.

YUCA con mojo

CASSAVA WITH CITRUS DRESSING

Serves 4–6

2 lb (900 g) yuca • ¼ cup (60 ml) vegetable oil • 1 red onion, finely chopped

3 garlic cloves, minced • 2 tsp fresh lime juice • 2 tsp salt • 1 pinch dried oregano

▷ Peel and wash the yuca. As you work, place the yuca in a bowl of cold water to keep from discoloring. Quarter the yuca lengthwise and cut into 4-inch (10-cm) pieces. Cut out the stringy core if necessary.

▷ Place the yuca in a pot, cover with water, and bring to a boil. Cook until soft but not falling apart, about 30 mins. If using a pressure cooker, bring it up to pressure and cook with 2 inches (5 cm) of water for 6–8 mins, followed by a quick release of the pressure valve according to manufacturer's instructions. Drain well.

▷ Heat the oil in a skillet over low heat. Sauté the onions until soft, 5–6 mins. Add the garlic and cook until softened but not browned, 1 min. Remove from heat and cool.

▷ Stir the lime juice, salt, and oregano into the onion mixture. (I usually shake everything together in a mason jar.) Pour over the yuca. Serve warm.

Puré de Malanga

MALANGA MASH • SERVES 4

This dish is a satisfying side starch for any Cuban meal, and is perhaps one of the most beloved comfort foods. When describing malanga, most people say it's pretty much like a potato, though longer and hairier (page 78). Some big differences include a higher protein content and more vitamins B and C, plus there's a general consensus that malanga aids in digestion. Puré de Malanga is also one of the most common baby foods in Cuba; it can be found year round in the markets and in food rations, especially those for small children.

▷ Salt
▷ 2 lb (900 g) malanga, peeled and cut into 2-inch (5-cm) pieces
▷ 2 Tbsp vegetable oil
▷ 4 garlic cloves, peeled and smashed
▷ 1/3 cup (80 ml) heavy cream (optional)
▷ Pepper

Fill a large pot 2/3 full with water, add 3-4 Tbsp salt and bring to a boil. Add malanga and cook until it can be easily pierced with a fork, about 15 mins. Drain, reserving 1 cup (240 ml) cooking liquid.

Heat oil in a pan over medium heat, add garlic, and sauté for 3-4 mins. Remove from the heat. Put malanga and reserved liquid into a food processor. Process until smooth, adding cream if you like, and salt and pepper to taste. Top with the garlicky oil and serve.

CALALÚ

Santería, a religion that is derived from African Yoruban ancestry, is widely practiced in Cuba, and it's not uncommon to see an offering on a doorstep—a dead bird in a bowl of water or candles and dishes of food by a doorway. Rich in myth and symbolism, this religion references over 200 *orishas* and *osha* (deities), each one devoted to specific themes.

Calalú is considered a favorite dish of the Santerian deity, Changó—and it is customary to prepare it when one wants to call on Changó to wish for good health. I love this dish for its wealth of green vegetables.

Greens Stew • Serves 4

1½ lb (775 g) mixed greens, such as kale, chard, yuca leaves, and purslane, chopped

2 tsp achiote oil (page 000)

1 bell pepper, diced

3—4 green onions, chopped

2—3 culantro leaves or 2—3 whole, fresh Cuban oregano leaves, minced (reserve some for garnish)

½ lb (230 g) protein of choice: fish, smoked pork, or chicken, cubed

Salt and pepper

6 Roma tomatoes, chopped

1 cup (240 ml) coconut milk

Steam the greens until tender, then drain and set aside. Heat the achiote oil in a large sauté pan. Add the bell pepper, green onions, and culantro or oregano and sauté for 5 mins. Add protein and cook until browned. Season to taste with salt and pepper and reduce heat to medium-low. Stir in the tomatoes, coconut milk, and steamed greens. Simmer the calalú until thickened, 10—15 mins. Garnish each serving with minced culantro or oregano.

Tortilla
de Berenjena con Maíz Tierno

EGGPLANT AND CORN OMELET
serves 6
This thick Cuban tortilla is of Spanish origin.
Try variations of vegetables in this recipe.

- 2 large eggplants, peeled and cut into 1-inch (2.5-cm) cubes
- Salt and pepper
- 6 Tbsp olive oil, divided
- 1 large onion, finely chopped
- 1 red bell pepper, thinly sliced
- 1 cup (175 g) fresh or frozen corn kernels
- 4 eggs
- 1 cup (240 ml) milk
- 1 cup (113 g) grated Gouda or Swiss cheese
- 1 tsp dried oregano

1. Soak the eggplant in a bowl of well-salted water for at least 30 mins. Place a plate over the eggplant to keep the pieces fully immersed. Rinse, then pat dry to extract as much moisture as possible.

2. Heat 3 Tbsp olive oil in a large frying pan over medium heat. Sauté eggplant for 5–8 mins, then add onions, bell pepper, and corn. Cook until tender, about 10 mins.

3. In a large mixing bowl, beat the 4 eggs. Add the milk, cheese, oregano, and sautéed vegetables. Season to taste with salt and pepper and mix well.

4. Heat the remaining 3 Tbsp olive oil in a clean frying pan, tipping it to coat the bottom and sides. Pour mixture into pan. Cook on medium heat until the edges of the egg begin to set, then reduce to medium-low. Shake the pan every so often to prevent the *tortilla* from sticking to the bottom. *Tortilla* should be fully cooked in about 12 mins. Let cool for at least 10 mins.

5. Invert a large plate over the top of the skillet. Using a hot pad, hold plate down firmly, and flip the skillet and plate. Lift the pan off of the plate and if all goes well, *tortilla* will be upside down on the plate. Slice the *tortilla* as you would a pie, and serve warm or at room temperature.

Crema de Berro
Cream of Watercress • Serves 6

When I first made this soup in the US after trying it at a paladar in Havana, my friend Juan commented how much it tasted like broccoli. That comment reminded me of a few fellow travelers who lamented how they missed this vegetable, which is not a common crop in Cuba. I wish I had suggested they satisfy their cravings with the more readily available watercress, also a member of the brassica family.

- 1 lb (450 g) potatoes, peeled
- 4 cups (940 ml) water, divided
- ¾ lb (340 g) watercress (about 2 bunches), chopped
- 5 Tbsp olive oil, divided
- ½ onion, minced
- 1 garlic clove, mashed
- 1 cup (240 ml) whole milk
- Salt and pepper to taste
- 1 tsp ground achiote
- Garnishes: Thinly sliced green onions and lime wedges

1. Boil the potatoes (or cook in a pressure cooker) until tender. When cool enough to handle, dice the potatoes into ½-inch (13-mm) pieces.

2. Bring 3 cups (700 ml) water to a boil. Add watercress and blanch for 1 min. Transfer the mixture to a blender along with half of the potatoes and blend until smooth.

3. Combine 3 Tbsp olive oil, onion, and garlic in a large pot and sauté over medium heat until soft.

4. Add watercress mixture to pot. Stir in the milk and remaining 1 cup (240 ml) water and cook over low heat for 15–20 mins. Add salt and pepper to taste.

5. Heat remaining 2 Tbsp olive oil in a skillet over medium heat. Stir in the achiote until dissolved (this lends color to the potatoes). Add the remaining diced potatoes and fry until crispy. Serve with garnishes.

ENSALADA de Tomates pintones

Semiripe Tomato Salad | SERVES 4

This is a very basic salad that is possible to prepare when tomatoes are almost in season. Rather than the ripe fruit to which we're all more accustomed, look for tomatoes that are firm, a bit tart, and crunchy—and savor the contrast.

> ¼ cup (60 ml) olive oil

> 2 Tbsp red wine vinegar

> Salt and pepper

> 1 medium white onion, thinly sliced

> 3—4 large semiripe tomatoes (pink and green)

Whisk together the oil, vinegar, 1 tsp salt and pepper to taste. Mix in the sliced onions and set aside for 20 minutes to marinate.

Using a sharp knife, peel and thinly slice the tomatoes. Arrange on a platter. Pour the dressed onions over the tomatoes and serve.

Variation: Instead of the dressing, sprinkle a combination of salt and sugar over the tomatoes and onions.

COL salteada

Sautéed Cabbage
Serves 4

This dish is served at room temperature. I use a mandoline for slicing the cabbage, which makes the slices really thin and uniform.

¼ cup (60 ml) oil
½ onion, thinly sliced
½ red bell pepper, thinly sliced
2 garlic cloves, mashed
1 Tbsp tomato paste
2 cups (200 g) thinly sliced cabbage
Salt and black pepper

Heat the oil in a skillet over medium-high heat. Add onions and cook until softened. Add red pepper and garlic and cook for 5 more minutes. Stir in the tomato paste. Add cabbage, stir well to combine, then cook covered, until cabbage is tender, 6–8 minutes. Season to taste with salt and pepper. Let cool to room temperature before serving.

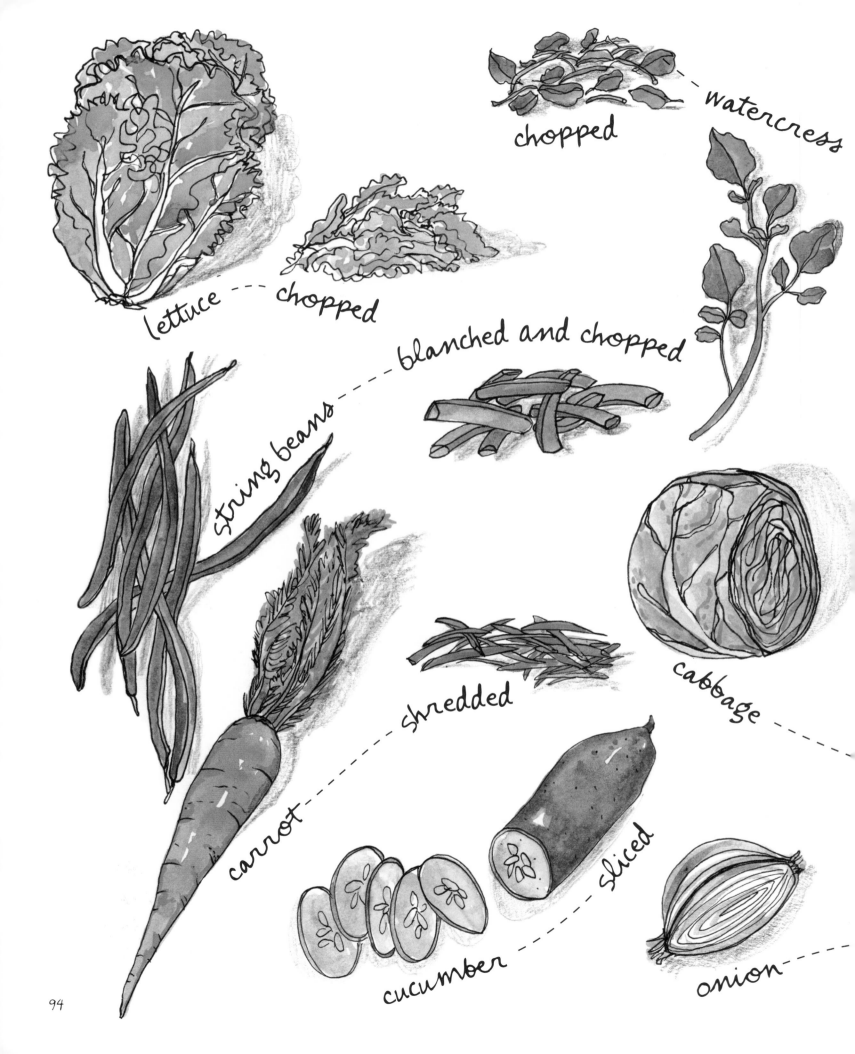

chopped

watercress

lettuce   chopped

blanched and chopped

string beans

cabbage

shredded

carrot

cucumber   sliced

onion

{ La Ensalada MIXTA }

Mixed Salad

On the Cuban table, along with a protein and a root vegetable, there is almost always an ensalada mixta, a salad with a citrus- or vinegar-based dressing (aliño).

This fresh dish varies with what is available—perhaps it is watercress with tomatoes and thinly sliced onions, or steamed green beans under a bed of sliced cabbage, carrots, and cucumbers. Mix and match your veggies, then make a good, all-purpose aliño by whisking together ¼ cup (60 ml) olive oil, 2 Tbsp white vinegar, 2 Tbsp fresh lime juice, and 1 tsp salt. Makes about ½ cup (120 ml) of dressing.

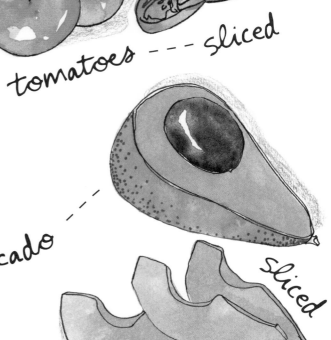

tomatoes --- sliced

shredded

Soak in cold water with 1 Tbsp salt for 20 mins.

thinly sliced

avocado

sliced

95

Cómo Cocinar
Huevos Duros Perfectos

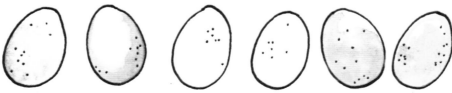

How to Make Perfect Hard-Boiled Eggs
Pro tip: Use week-old eggs for best results.

1.

Insert steaming rack into pot and fill with 1 inch (2.5 cm) warm water.

2.

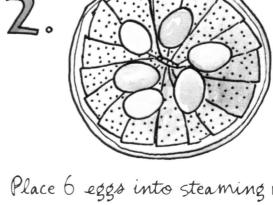

Place 6 eggs into steaming rack.

3.

Cover, bring water to a simmer, and steam for 20 mins on medium-low heat.

4.

Place eggs in colander and rinse until cool to the touch.

5.

Peel and enjoy.

ENSALADA RUSA

Russian Potato Salad
Serves 4–6

The USSR became Cuba's main trade partner in the second half of the 20th century, and the majority of Cuba's imports came from the Soviets in exchange, most often, for sugar. The two countries remained great allies up until the Soviet collapse of 1989. From Soviet-style architecture to cuisine, the communist country certainly left its mark on Cuba. Fun fact: The USSR invited Cuban-born Amaldo Tamayo Méndez to join its 1980 intercosmos program; he became the first person of African descent in space and represented the ninth country in space.

- 4–6 red potatoes, peeled and cubed
- 2 hard-boiled eggs, chopped
- 1 small onion, minced
- 8-oz (230-g) jar roasted pimentos, minced
- 8 oz (230 g) frozen peas, blanched

- ¾ cup (180 ml) mayonnaise
- 1 Tbsp olive oil
- 1 Tbsp red wine vinegar
- Salt and pepper to taste

Boil the potatoes in a pot of salted water over medium heat until tender, 12–15 mins. Drain and cool.

Combine the potatoes, eggs, onion, pimentos, and peas in a large bowl (reserve a couple of spoonfuls of peas and pimentos for garnish). Gently stir in the mayonnaise, olive oil, and vinegar and season with salt and pepper to taste. Garnish with the reserved peas and pimentos.

Ensalada de Col

con vegetales mixtos

Cabbage Salad with Mixed Vegetables
Serves 8

- 1 small cabbage, thinly sliced
- 2 carrots, cut into matchsticks
- 1 bunch watercress leaves
- ¼ cup (60 ml) olive oil
- 3 Tbsp white vinegar
- 1 Tbsp fresh lime juice
- 1 tsp sugar
- ½ tsp salt
- Pepper to taste
- 2 English cucumbers, sliced lengthwise then rolled up
- 2 tomatoes, cut into wedges
- 2–3 cooked beets, sliced
- 1 avocado, sliced

1. In a bowl, combine the cabbage, carrots, and watercress.
2. Whisk together the olive oil, vinegar, lime juice, sugar, salt, and pepper. Add half of the dressing to the vegetables and mix well. Garnish the salad around the edges with the tomatoes, beets, cucumber, and avocado. Pour the remainder of the dressing on top. Serve immediately.

ENSALADA de PIÑA y AGUACATE

Pineapple & Avocado Salad

SERVES 6

Try grilling the pineapple first to boost its flavor.

- ¼ cup (60 mL) olive oil
- 3 Tbsp white vinegar
- 3 Tbsp fresh orange juice
- 1 tsp salt
- ½ tsp pepper

- 2 cups (330 g) fresh pineapple slices
- 1 large bunch watercress
- 1 small red onion, thinly sliced
- 1 ripe avocado, sliced

- Whisk together the olive oil, vinegar, orange juice, salt, and pepper; set aside.

- In a large bowl or a platter, combine the pineapple, watercress, and onion. Add half of the dressing and toss gently. Add the avocado and pour the rest of the dressing over the salad.

Algunas FRUTAS de Cuba

Some Fruit of Cuba

In Cuba, most fruit is eaten fresh and at its peak in season. Additionally, you'll find it whirred in a blender to make a fresh batido (milkshake), added to cocktails, or used to flavor homemade helado (ice cream). Here are some of the more unusual varieties I came across:

MAMEY SAPOTE

Fruit is sweet, rich, creamy, pink flesh, often served in a milkshake or ice cream.

NARANJA AGRIA

Sour Orange
This tart citrus is the more traditional acid to use in mojo sauce.

GUINEO

Also known as banana manzano, this little banana is eaten fresh.

CHERIMOYA

Custard Apple
Peel and enjoy the white fruit, avoiding seeds; best eaten fresh.

NÍSPERO

Loquat
This sweet-tart stone fruit is commonly eaten fresh.

CAIMITO

Star Apple
Cut this fruit in half to reveal a star in the center; enjoy fresh.

GRANADA

Pomegranate
Peel skin and eat the concentrated sweet seeds; juice also used in cocktails.

GUANABANA

Soursop
Creamy and tropical flavor makes a great fresh juice.

GUAYABA

Guava
Pink-orange flesh with small seeds that should be strained when making juice or ice cream.

CIRUELA CHINA

Chinese Plum
This small purple and yellow plum is tart and sweet, seasonal in Cuba.

MAMONCILLO

Spanish Lime
Peel away the hard green shell to reveal edible, pink flesh.

ANÓN

Custard Apple
Sweet and fragrant with a knobby section that separates when ripe.

CANISTEL

Closely related to the lucuma or eggfruit, it has a somewhat thick and dry consistency when blended.

Jugos
FRESCOS
Fresh Juice

You can make juice from any combination of fruit you like. The ratio to remember is 1 cup (175 g) chopped fruit to 1½ cups (350 ml) water plus 1 Tbsp sugar (optional), and the key is to prepare the juice when the fruit is at its peak ripeness.

Try:

Papaya

Pineapple

Soursop
guanabana

Mamey Sapote

Wash, peel, and chop enough fruit to measure about 1 cup (175 g).
Add the fruit to a blender, along with 1 Tbsp sugar or to taste.
Blend to a smooth purée.
Add 1½ cups (350 ml) water and blend again.
If you like, strain the juice, discarding any fibrous pulp. Refrigerate until ready to serve.
This recipe can be doubled or tripled.

Cómo Cortar una Piña

How to Cut Up a Pineapple

1.

Begin by twisting off the top leaves, then cut off the bottom to make a flat surface.

2.

Hold the pineapple upright; slice off the peel.

3.

Slice into rounds.

4.

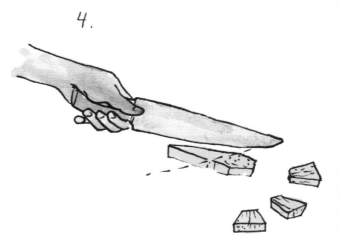

Cut into bite-size pieces, discarding the dense core in the center of each slice.

GARAPIÑA

Fermented Pineapple Juice

In the eastern part of Cuba, this drink is called chicha. Tart, fizzy, and a little sweet, it makes a refreshing treat on a hot day. The sugars become slightly fermented, producing probiotics that are good for your gut, but if your batch of garapiña sits out too long, it will eventually turn into vinegar. Add sugar at the very end, then refrigerate to slow the fermentation.

Serves 4

Peels from 1 pineapple
4–6 cups (950–1,425 ml) boiling water
Sugar to taste

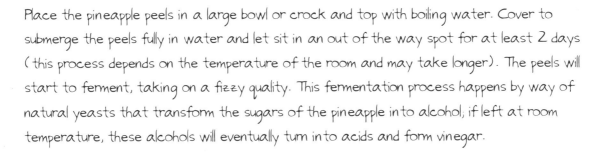

Place the pineapple peels in a large bowl or crock and top with boiling water. Cover to submerge the peels fully in water and let sit in an out of the way spot for at least 2 days (this process depends on the temperature of the room and may take longer). The peels will start to ferment, taking on a fizzy quality. This fermentation process happens by way of natural yeasts that transform the sugars of the pineapple into alcohol; if left at room temperature, these alcohols will eventually turn into acids and form vinegar.

When the liquid has reached the desired fizziness, strain and discard the peels. Stir in sugar to taste.

Refrigerate the garapiña and serve over ice.

Variations:
• Try mixing with orange juice, a bit of lime juice, and a touch of cinnamon.
• Stir some of the garapiña with rum and crushed ice to make a cocktail.

Home Remedies in CUBA

Remedios Caseros en Cuba

Despite the fact that Cuba provides its citizens with free healthcare, offers free medical school education for potential doctors, and has one of the strongest medical research programs in the world, access to a pharmacy can be difficult in rural areas. The Cuban spirit of *resolver* (page 13) welcomes the idea of home remedies to bridge this gap.

Time-honored homeopathic and herbal cures are a cost-effective way to treat simple ailments and help fill the void left by the shortage of medicines. Efforts to teach and utilize natural healing methods continue. It is said that there's *un cocimiento* (an herbal concoction) to cure just about any ailment, and herbal teas, tinctures, and salves are made in the home to battle a cough, rash, and various other sicknesses.

PRÚ

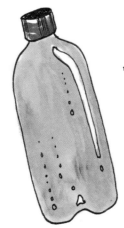

Traditionally prepared in the eastern provinces of Cuba, *prú* is a refreshing homemade fermented brew that is said to have medicinal properties. It is touted to be an aphrodisiac, high in antioxidants, and may even lower blood pressure. *Prú* arrived to the island with the influx of French sugar plantation owners and their slaves after the Haitian revolution at the end of the 18th century. It is made of roots and spices, including chinaberry, *ñame* root, *jaboncillo* (soap tree roots), ginger, pine tree shoots, cinnamon sticks, lemongrass, and sugar, that are boiled then strained. When cool, the liquid is combined with a mother from a previous batch of *prú* and set to ferment for two days. Afterwards the *prú* is bottled, with some saved as the mother for the next batch.

I had my theories about the drink after talking at length with social scientist and Baracoan native, Invalis Guilbeaux Rodríguez, and after trying it and enjoying a whole glass, I was convinced—it's the Cuban kombucha. Be careful when opening a bottle, as it is very fizzy!

Herbs in the Home

Hierbas en el Hogar

Cuban locals often pointed out alternate uses for ingredients while we were shopping in markets or cooking. I gained an understanding of some of the common medicinal uses for herbs and spices we were frequently tossing into the *cazuela*.

MIEL

Honey's viscosity can help provide a protective barrier to prevent infection for wounds and can also be used as a cough suppressant. It also helps to fight canker sores. Clean infected area with a sterile cloth or cotton ball, then dab a little honey directly on the sore. Repeat as needed, to mete out sweet revenge!

OREGANO

Oregano oil is considered an anti-inflammatory, antifungal, and antibacterial agent, as well as a natural pain reliever. The oil can be taken orally for a cough, cold, aches and pains, or digestive issues.

Isabel taught me how to make oregano oil: Heat equal parts olive oil and muddled fresh oregano over low heat for about 1 min (heat aids the infusion process). Strain leaves and discard. Store oil in a jar in a cool, dark place for up to 4 weeks.

MANTECA de CACAO

Rich in antioxidants, fresh cocoa butter is used to moisturize skin, lips, and hair and combat wrinkles and the appearance of scars. Because it is completely natural and free of fragrance and coloring, manteca de cacao is great for those with sensitive skin. This plant-derived saturated fat contains properties that reduce the risk of cardiovascular diseases. If you're cooking with it, just be aware that it is high in calories!

CAÑA SANTA

To alleviate a cough or stomachache, steep 1—2 Tbsp minced fresh lemongrass (packed in a tea ball or tied in cotton cloth) in 1 cup (240 ml) hot water and drink as tea. This tea is also said to reduce blood pressure.

AJO

Garlic is an antifungal agent and antioxidant, and has been proven to boost immunity and fight congestion: boil about 8 cups (2 L) water in a large pot and add 3—5 smashed garlic cloves. Remove from heat. Place a towel over your head and lean over the pot, keeping your face at least 6 inches (15 cm) from the pot. Breathe deeply for 5—10 mins, allowing the steam to enter your lungs.

EN LA CAFETERIA

In the Café

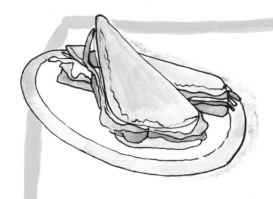

Café a Todas Horas

Coffee at All Hours

In the *cafeterías* (lunch counters) of Cuba, there are several things that you can order morning, noon, or night, including sandwiches, *empanadas*, and my favorite, *croquetas*. And, not to be overlooked, coffee is an essential element of every day for most Cubans.

In addition to making it at home in a *cafetera* (Italian moka pot), people stop by *ventanitas* to get their coffee fix while out and about. These little windows are often located on the side of a *cafetería* facing the sidewalk so anyone can stop for a few minutes, talk to a *vecino* (neighbor), and enjoy a *café* at any hour of the day.

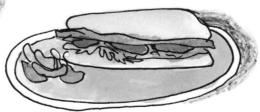

Café Cubano

Also known as cafecito, this refers to a shot of coffee usually drawn with sugar and served in an espresso cup. It is sweet, strong, and somewhat viscous because of the sugar. If made in a cafetera (the way many Cubans make coffee at home), it is often brewed with sugar.

Colada

Found frequently in the streets of Miami, this is the family-style cafecito: a colada contains 4–6 shots of espresso and is served along with tiny to-go plastic cups; individual potions are doled out in these small containers to family members, coworkers, and friends.

Café del Campo

This is the old-school way to make coffee; traditionally the way people make coffee in the countryside. This method uses a manga (net or thin fabric) supported by a stand placed over the coffeepot. Hot water is poured over the grounds, and the café passes through. As the café brews, the grounds are swirled using a wooden paddle, and the net is twisted using the paddle, pushing the liquid through.

Café con Leche

A cafecito with steamed or warm milk. It's often served as a cup of sweetened espresso with a small pitcher of milk, so one can add desired quantity of milk. Café con leche is a favorite especially during breakfast with pan tostado and pasta de guayaba (guava paste) or even tostones.

Cortadito

A cafecito cut with a bit of steamed milk. This drink is smoother than a straight cafecito—because it contains milk—and is similar to café con leche but with less milk. The only difference between this and the Italian cortado is that the cortadito is presweetened.

Cómo se Usa una Cafetera
How to Use a Moka Coffeepot

1.

Unscrew the moka pot and remove the funnel.

2.

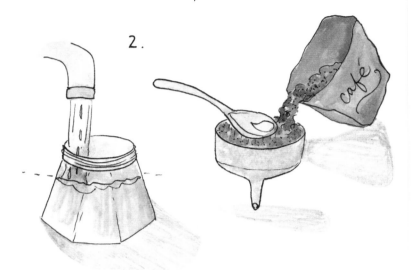

Fill the lower section with cold water just below the insert. Fill the funnel with fine-ground espresso and level off with spoon, but do not pack down. Place funnel in the base of the pot.

3.

Screw the upper chamber onto the base tightly and light stove.

4.

Place pot on the stovetop over medium heat, until the water boils and coffee bubbles to the upper chamber. Serve hot!

PASTELITOS

Puff Pastry Pies • Makes 16

Pastelitos, or little pies, are sweet or savory, traditionally filled with Picadillo (page 38), guava paste, or cream cheese. This recipe is fun because it's quick to make, and the outcome looks a lot more complicated than it actually is. Puff pastry dough can be found in the frozen foods section of most grocery stores. In Cuba, the pastelitos are often larger than the ones in this recipe, and may be round or triangular. I find making them as squares is easier because there's no leftover dough.

- 1 (17.3-oz/490-g) pkg frozen puff pastry, thawed
- Flour, for dusting
- ½ cup (150g) guava paste, cream cheese, or Picadillo (page 38)
- Egg wash: 1 egg beaten well with 1 tsp water
- Simple syrup: ¼ cup (50 g) sugar stirred into ¼ cup (60 ml) boiling water until dissolved

▷ Preheat the oven to 400°F (204°C).

▷ Place 1 sheet of puff pastry on a clean surface and sprinkle both sides with flour. Using a sharp knife, cut the pastry into 16 squares. Repeat with the 2nd sheet of puff pastry.

▷ Arrange half of the squares on a nonstick cookie sheet. Place about 2 tsp of filling in the center of each square. Brush the edges with egg wash and top with another square. Press the edges together and use a fork to seal in a decorative manner. Make 1 or 2 small slits on the top of each pastry, then brush with egg wash.

▷ Bake until golden brown, about 20 mins. Remove from the oven and brush the pastries lightly with simple syrup (omit the syrup if filled with picadillo or other savory filling).

Fritters lend themselves well to using up leftovers, and therefore there are many variations. This calabaza fritters recipe is on the sweeter side of things, and the malanga recipe, more savory. Both are vegetarian.

FRIT

de Malanga

MALANGA FRITTERS • SERVES 4-6

When chef Lázaro Chirino Padrón cooked with me in my kitchen in Havana, he brought over his handmade grater for fritura prep. His trusty tool—a thick sheet of metal perforated with nail holes and secured to a small wooden frame—did the trick beautifully.

MALANGA

- 1 egg
- 1 garlic clove, minced
- 1 tsp chopped parsley
- 1 tsp salt
- 1 lb (450 g) malanga, peeled and shredded
- 1 cup (240 ml) vegetable oil
- ½ cup (120 ml) honey, for dipping

In a mixing bowl, beat the egg well. Mix in the garlic, parsley, and salt. Add the shredded malanga and stir well to combine.

Heat oil in a skillet to 375°F (191°C). Gently drop 1-Tbsp scoops of the batter into the hot oil and fry, turning once, until golden brown. Drain on paper towels and serve hot with a small bowl of honey.

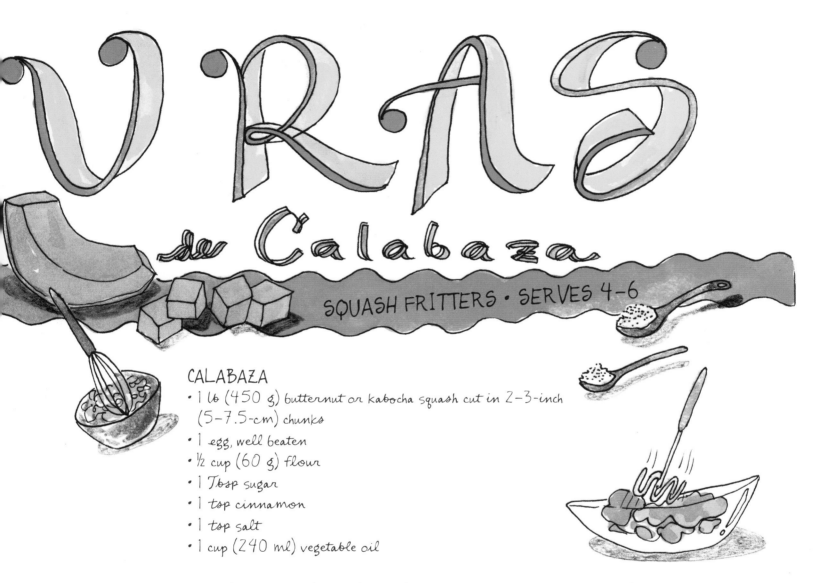

VRAS de Calabaza

SQUASH FRITTERS · SERVES 4-6

CALABAZA
- 1 lb (450 g) butternut or kabocha squash cut in 2-3-inch (5-7.5-cm) chunks
- 1 egg, well beaten
- ½ cup (60 g) flour
- 1 Tbsp sugar
- 1 tsp cinnamon
- 1 tsp salt
- 1 cup (240 ml) vegetable oil

Steam the **calabaza** with ½ cup (120 ml) water until tender. This will take 15–20 mins on the stovetop or about 8 mins in a pressure cooker. Let cool to room temperature, then peel.

Mash the **calabaza** with a potato masher or fork until it is a smooth purée. Stir in the egg, flour, sugar, cinnamon, and salt to make a batter.

Heat oil in a skillet. Gently drop 1-Tbsp scoops of the batter into the hot oil and fry, turning once, until golden. Drain on paper towels and serve hot.

CROQUETTES • MAKES ABOUT 30

Isabel González and María Magdalena Domínguez, my landlord and neighbor in central Havana, taught me how to make croquetas. Isabel worked for several years in a busy cafetería (lunch counter), where she prepared croquetas almost every day. Croquetas can be formed and breaded up to 6 hours ahead and refrigerated, then fried right before serving. This afternoon of cooking was particularly memorable because we listened to the loud TV from the other room, as President Obama addressed the Cuban people in a special broadcast during his first visit to Cuba. At that moment, the feeling of economic change throughout the country was palpable.

▷ ¼ cup (56 g) butter
▷ ½ cup (75 g) finely minced onion
▷ 1½ cups (180 g) flour, plus more for dredging
▷ 1 cup (240 ml) warm milk
▷ 1 Tbsp vino seco (dry white wine)
▷ 1 tsp salt
▷ ½ tsp cumin
▷ ¼ tsp ground black pepper
▷ 1 lb (450 g) smoked ham, minced in a food processor*
▷ 4 eggs, lightly beaten
▷ 2 cups (80 g) cracker crumbs or fresh bread crumbs
▷ 2 cups (475 ml) vegetable oil for frying

1. Melt butter in a caldero (or heavy saucepan), add onion, and sauté until just translucent. Add flour, stirring constantly, then pour in the warm milk and vino seco. Add salt, cumin, and pepper and cook at low heat, stirring constantly, until the mixture reaches a thick pastelike consistency, 5–10 mins. Fold in the minced ham and cook for another 2–4 mins or so. When the batter begins to pull away from the sides of the saucepan, remove from heat and cool for 1 hour in the refrigerator.

2. Divide the mixture into 1-Tbsp portions, put a little oil on your hands to keep the dough from sticking, and roll into desired shape (typically croquetas are round or oblong). Dip a croqueta in the beaten egg, dredge in flour, then shake excess off. Dip it again in the egg then roll it in the cracker crumbs. Cover all the croquetas this way, replenishing flour and bread crumbs if necessary.

3. Heat about 2 inches (5 cm) oil in a skillet to 370°F (188°C). Working in batches, fry the croquetas, turning them until they are golden brown on all sides, 2–3 mins. Using a slotted spoon, transfer to paper towels to drain. Be sure to bring temperature back to 370°F (188°C) for each batch. Keep the finished croquetas warm until all frying is finished. Serve with ketchup and mayonnaise.

*Variation: Use shredded cooked chicken instead of ham.

BATIDOS

MILKSHAKES

IN CUBA, PEOPLE ENJOY BATIDOS
MORNING, NOON, AND NIGHT.
I PREFER TO USE FROZEN FRUIT,
WHICH MAKES FOR A NICE COLD SHAKE.

SERVES 2–4

2 cups (475 ml) milk
2 cups (350 g) chopped fruit, frozen, such as
anón, mamey, guanábana (page 100), or papaya
¼ cup (50 g) sugar or to taste
2 cups (215 g) ice

Combine all ingredients
in a blender and blend well.
Serve at once.

EMPANADAS

Makes 10–12

Turnovers

Homemade empanadas in Cuba can be sweet or savory and often have a large fanlike border created by pressing a fork around the edges. Picadillo is the traditional savory filling, but also try using marmalade, cream cheese, or a combination of both for a sweet snack to enjoy with a café cubano.

> 2 cups (240 g) all-purpose flour

> 1 tsp sugar

> 1 tsp baking powder

> ½ tsp salt

> 4 Tbsp chilled shortening, cut into pieces

> 2 Tbsp chilled butter, cut into pieces

> 1 large egg, plus 1 egg yolk

> ½ cup (120 ml) cold water, or as needed

> 2 cups (400 g) Picadillo (page 38), for filling

> Vegetable oil, for frying

1. Combine the flour, sugar, baking powder, and salt in a food processor and pulse a few times to blend. Add the shortening and butter and pulse until the mixture is crumbly. Lightly beat the whole egg and yolk together and add to the processor; pulse until just combined. With the processor running, add the water, little by little, until the dough just comes together. It should be soft and pliable like pie dough. Transfer to a bowl, cover, and refrigerate for about 30 mins.

2. Divide the dough into 3 pieces. Working with 1 piece at a time (refrigerate the rest), roll the dough out on a lightly floured work surface into a thin round. Using a large can or saucer as a guide, cut the dough into 6-inch (15-cm) rounds. Repeat with the remaining dough. Spoon 2 Tbsp picadillo on the lower half of each round. Using your fingers, moisten the edges of the round and fold over to enclose the filling. Seal the edges by pressing with your fingers or a fork.

3. Heat ½ inch (13 mm) vegetable oil in a large, deep skillet to about 370°F (188°C). Working in batches, fry the empanadas until golden brown, 2–3 mins per side. Using a slotted spoon, transfer the empanadas to a paper towel-lined plate to drain. Serve immediately.

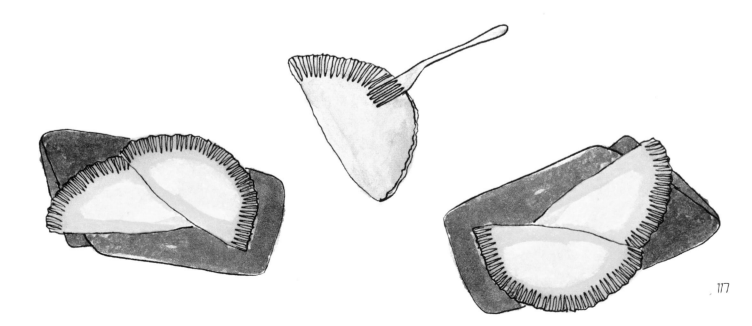

SÁNDWICH Elena Ruz

Serves 1

A young woman from the Vedado neighborhood of Havana invented this unique sandwich in the 1920s. She frequented a restaurant called El Carmelo in her neighborhood and would often request this creative combination. Eventually, the sandwich found its way onto the menu there, and then gained widespread popularity in Havana. Many Cuban diners began to offer it, and it remains a favorite almost a century later.

1 Medianoche BUN (SWEET EGG BREAD)
CREAM CHEESE
STRAWBERRY JAM
SLICED ROASTED TURKEY
BUTTER

Slice the bun in half. Spread a generous amount of cream cheese on one side and strawberry jam on the other. Place the turkey slices in between. Butter the outside of the bun on both sides. Cook in a hot skillet topped with a weight, flipping halfway through, until golden brown (or grill in a panini press).

SÁNDWICH CUBANO

Contrary to popular belief, the Cuban sandwich is not an authentic Cuban dish but a signature sandwich served at many Tampa and Miami lunch counters. A take on the sandwich mixto that can be found all over Cuba, el Cubano is an invention of Cuban migrant workers who worked in the cigar and sugar industries in south Florida. They folded roast pork, ham, Swiss cheese, pickles, and even salami into lengths of Cuban bread—a nod to Italian laborers in the area at the turn of the 20th century. These days, you'll find variations of the sandwich, including the addition of Croquetas (page 114) called the croqueta preparada, and its sweet sister sandwich, La Medianoche, described below.

Makes 4 sandwiches

- 1 loaf Cuban bread (about 18-inches/46-cm long)
- 2 Tbsp butter, softened
- 2 Tbsp yellow mustard
- 6 slices dill pickles
- 8 slices Swiss cheese
- 6 slices boiled ham
- 6 slices roast pork (page 24)

Slice the loaf of bread lengthwise and butter the outside. Spread mustard lightly inside the bread, and add pickles. Place 4 slices of cheese over the pickles then top with the ham, pork, and remaining cheese. Close up the loaf and cut into quarters. Grill on both sides at low temperature until cheese is melted and bread is slightly golden. Alternatively, place the sandwich in a cast-iron frying pan, top with foil, and press with a weight (a brick wrapped with foil works great).

La Medianoche

Change out the Cuban bread for a sweet egg bread. This bread is similar to a challah bread. Toast it, and you've got the sweeter version of the classic, called La Medianoche.

POSTRES

Desserts

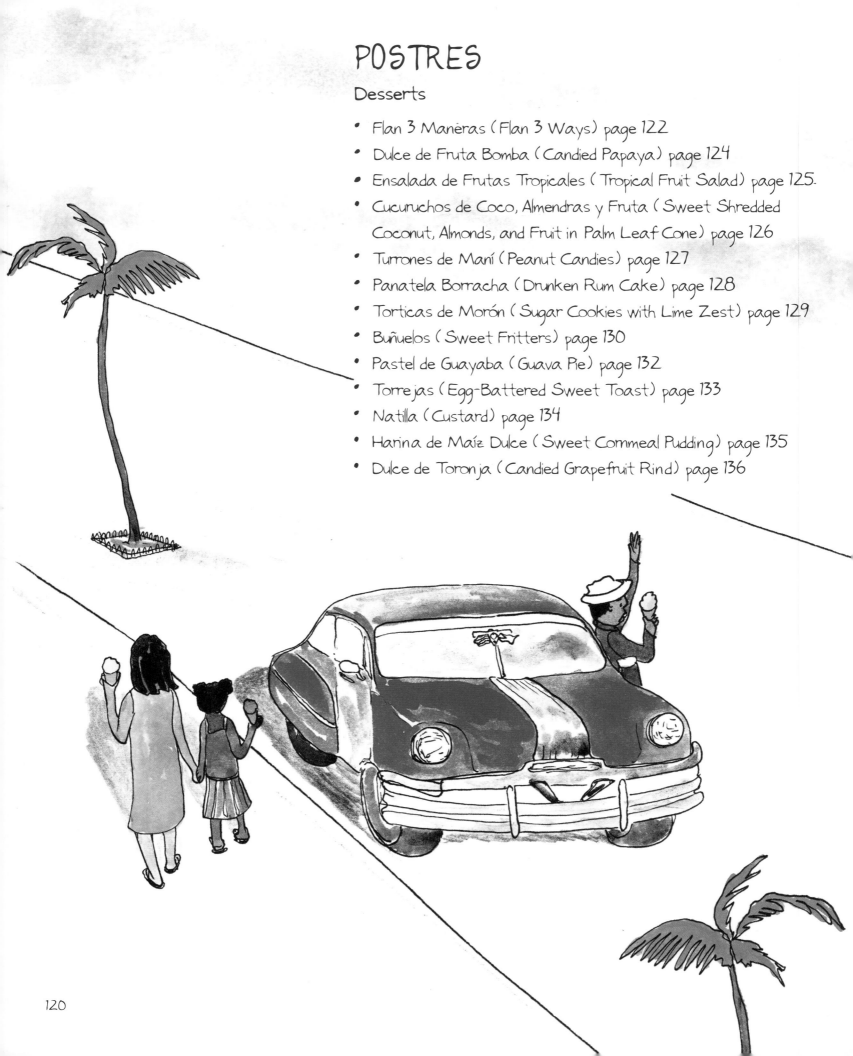

Siempre Hay Algo Dulce

There's Always Something Sweet

For centuries, Cuba was considered "the world's sugar bowl." From the arrival of the Spanish in the 15th century, when they established sugarcane crops, until the present, sugar has reigned supreme and has been the country's primary export commodity. In 1970, Fidel Castro challenged the people of Cuba to cultivate their largest production ever, proposing the 10 Million–Ton Sugar Harvest, a goal set to fulfill trade agreements with the Soviet Union. Although this goal wasn't quite met, it still remains the largest harvest to date. Since then, the production of sugar has been in decline, but it's still one of the country's largest exports.

Sugar is readily available within the country, and Cubans have always had quite a sweet tooth. They offer a variety of delicious desserts, utilizing the many tropical fruits and nuts grown on the island, to make recipes ranging from Pastel de Guayaba (Guava Pie), page 132 to Turrones de Maní (Peanut Candies), page 127. Ice cream, in a multitude of flavors, has to be the most popular Cuban treat, and most cities, regardless of size, feature at least one ice cream parlor. One of the uniquely Cuban flavors is called mantecado, a rich, egg yolk–based ice cream with a distinctive yellow color. I gained a new appreciation for the icy dessert while visiting in the sweltering heat of August. Between the presweetened café cubanos to the stewed fruit in syrup served with fresh cheese, I always found a way to satisfy my sugar cravings.

I've made flan countless times over the years, but preparing this dish in Cuba was a new experience entirely, because we made it in a pressure cooker. The whole process took less than 20 minutes! First prepare the caramel, then the flan mixture, and choose your method of cooking below.

Caramel:
1¼ cups (250 g) sugar
¼ cup (60 ml) water

Flan:
4 eggs
1 cup (240 ml) whole milk
1 tsp vanilla

Caramel: Combine ¾ cup (150 g) sugar and the water in a saucepan. Cook over medium heat until sugar dissolves and turns a medium to dark caramel color (10–15 mins). Stir every minute or so to keep from burning. Pour the caramel into a round mold or six 6-oz (180-ml) ramekins and swirl around to cover the bottom and sides.

Flan: Combine eggs, milk, vanilla, and remaining ½ cup (50 g) sugar in a blender and blend until very smooth. Pour into mold(s).

Method: Cook in either a water bath or a pressure cooker (see opposite page). When the flan has cooled, refrigerate, covered with plastic wrap for at least 4 hrs or overnight. When ready to serve, run a knife around the edge, place a large plate on top, and invert.

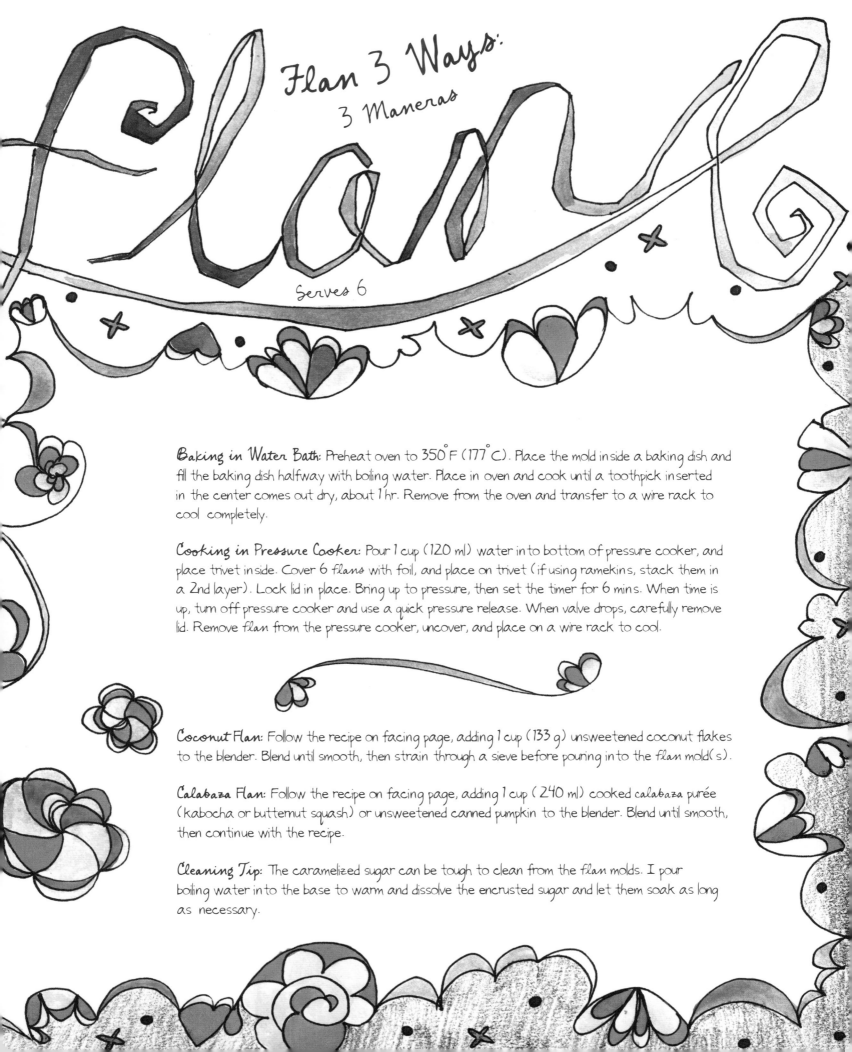

Flan 3 Ways:
3 Maneras

Serves 6

Baking in Water Bath: Preheat oven to 350°F (177°C). Place the mold inside a baking dish and fill the baking dish halfway with boiling water. Place in oven and cook until a toothpick inserted in the center comes out dry, about 1 hr. Remove from the oven and transfer to a wire rack to cool completely.

Cooking in Pressure Cooker: Pour 1 cup (120 ml) water into bottom of pressure cooker, and place trivet inside. Cover 6 *flans* with foil, and place on trivet (if using ramekins, stack them in a 2nd layer). Lock lid in place. Bring up to pressure, then set the timer for 6 mins. When time is up, turn off pressure cooker and use a quick pressure release. When valve drops, carefully remove lid. Remove *flan* from the pressure cooker, uncover, and place on a wire rack to cool.

Coconut Flan: Follow the recipe on facing page, adding 1 cup (133 g) unsweetened coconut flakes to the blender. Blend until smooth, then strain through a sieve before pouring into the *flan* mold(s).

Calabaza Flan: Follow the recipe on facing page, adding 1 cup (240 ml) cooked *calabaza* purée (kabocha or butternut squash) or unsweetened canned pumpkin to the blender. Blend until smooth, then continue with the recipe.

Cleaning Tip: The caramelized sugar can be tough to clean from the *flan* molds. I pour boiling water into the base to warm and dissolve the encrusted sugar and let them soak as long as necessary.

Dulce de Fruta Bomba

Candied Papaya • Serves 6–8

For my first recipe learned in Cuba, Carol and I walked to the corner produce market and bought everything that we needed, except for the sugar, which I had picked up the day before at the government-run supermarket. Make sure you select a firm, unripe papaya for this; when you shake the fruit, you shouldn't hear the seeds bouncing around inside.

1 large green, unripe papaya (about 2 lb/900 g)
6½ cups water, divided
2 cups (400 g) sugar
1-inch (2.5-cm) strip lime peel
1-inch (2.5-cm) strip orange peel
1 cinnamon stick
8 oz (230 g) cream cheese or Gouda cheese, for serving

1. Peel the papaya, remove the seeds, and cut the fruit into 2-inch (5-cm) chunks; rinse.

2. Place papaya and water in a pressure cooker, bring to pressure, and cook for 5 mins. (Or simmer in a pot until tender, about 20 mins.)

3. After the papaya is soft, transfer it to a heavy pot. Add sugar, 2½ cups (600 ml) water, citrus peels, and cinnamon stick to the pot and cook over medium heat. Stirring occasionally, cook until syrup starts to thicken, then reduce heat to low and simmer until syrup is somewhat reduced, about 1 hr.

4. Using a slotted spoon, scoop the cooked papaya onto a plate. Cut the cheese into 1x½-inch (25x13-mm) pieces and arrange around the papaya. Pick up a piece of cheese and a piece of the papaya with a fork and enjoy!

Ensalada de Frutas Tropicales

Tropical Fruit Salad
Serves 6

Simple Syrup:
- ½ cup (50 g) sugar
- ½ cup (120 ml) water
- ¼ cup (60 ml) fresh lime juice
- Zest of 1 lime
- Pinch of salt

Salad:
- Zest of 1 orange
- 2 large mangos, peeled and cut into chunks
- 2 oranges, peeled and sliced
- 1 papaya, seeded, peeled, and cut into chunks
- 1 pineapple, peeled, and cut into chunks

To make the syrup, heat sugar and water until sugar is dissolved. Stir in lime juice, citrus zest, and salt. Cool completely.

Combine all the fruit in a large bowl. Add the cooled syrup and refrigerate for at least 3 hrs before serving.

Note: The simple syrup is optional. In place of it, stir ½ cup (50 g) sugar into the fruit and refrigerate overnight before serving. Or omit sweetener all together!

The road from Moa to Baracoa was a bumpy ride—uneven and full of potholes. We stopped at a small stand on the city's outskirts, where I had heard people would be selling lo local, the distinct dishes made on the eastern tip of the island, including a dessert I had heard so much about. The vendor kindly gave me my first taste of cucurucho, a sticky mixture of freshly grated coconut, pineapple, honey, and almonds, which grow wild in Baracoa, presented in a palm leaf cone. She, like many, was also selling turrones de maní (candied peanuts), which are one of the most common snacks you'll see sold de manera callejera (by way of the streets). The peanut vendor melody, "El Manisero," ran through my mind. This song, a precursor to the rumba craze, was recorded by Antonio Machín in 1930 and was one of the biggest hits to have come out of Cuba.

CUCURUCHOS
de COCO, ALMENDRAS y FRUTA

SWEET SHREDDED COCONUT, ALMONDS, AND FRUIT IN PALM LEAF CONE

MAKES 12—14 CONES

- 1 cup (142 g) raw almonds • 3 cups (340 g) freshly shredded coconut (or packaged unsweetened coconut) • 5 cups (12 dL) water
- ½ cup (50 g) sugar • ½ cup (120 ml) honey
- ¼ cup (40 g) finely chopped fresh guava or pineapple
- Palm leaves or parchment paper

1. Spread the almonds on a cookie sheet and bake at 350°F (177°C) until golden, about 10 mins. Be careful not to burn. Set aside to cool.

2. Combine the coconut and water in a heavy pot and boil over medium heat until the coconut is soft and the mixture is thick, 35—40 mins.

3. Add the sugar and honey to the coconut, along with the fruit. Lower the heat and continue to cook the mixture, stirring frequently, until the coconut begins to turn a golden color, about 30 mins. Remove from heat and cool.

4. To make the cones: cut out triangles of palm leaf or parchment paper that are 6x15 inches (15x38 cm) and roll them into tapered cones, folding the loose end into the cone to secure it.

5. With a small spoon, fill each cone with the mixture.

Maní... Maní...
Si te quieres por el pico divertir
cómete un cucuruchito de maní...

EL MANISE

TURRONES de MANÍ

PEANUT CANDIES

Traveling around Cuba, I always had a turrón de maní in my bag. This great source of protein is, practically speaking, the Cuban energy bar. I learned to shape them on wet newspaper, but wax paper makes a good alternative.

- 5 cups (710 g) peeled raw peanuts
- 1½ cups (350 ml) water
- 2½ cups (533g) brown sugar
- 1 tsp salt
- 1 tsp baking soda
- Wax paper

1. Toast the peanuts in a heavy pot over medium-high heat, stirring constantly, until fragrant and beginning to turn a light brown color, about 15 mins. Remove peanuts from the pot and set aside.

2. Add the water to the pot and bring to just below a simmer. Add sugar and salt and cook, stirring constantly, as the sugar dissolves, bubbles, and turns golden. Add the toasted peanuts and the baking powder. Continue to stir constantly as the peanut mixture darkens, thickens into a sticky syrup, and caramelizes, 20–30 mins. To test the consistency, use 2 spoons to gather enough of the mixture to form a 2-inch (5-cm) mound. Place it on a wax paper–lined tray, the turrón should hold its shape. If not, continue to cook the mixture until thickened further.

3. When thick enough, form the turrones the same way, working carefully, as the sugar is very hot. Let cool completely before peeling them off the paper. Turrones will keep up to 2 weeks in a storage container.

SIDE A
THE PEANUT VENDOR
"El Manisero"

PANATELA
BORRACHA

DRUNKEN RUM CAKE • Serves 10-12

CAKE:

½ tsp salt
2 cups (240 g) all-purpose flour
2 tsp baking powder
6 egg whites

1 cup (200 g) sugar
12 egg yolks
1 tsp vanilla

SYRUP:

1½ cup (350 ml) water
3 cups (600 g) sugar
1-inch (2.5-cm) strip lemon zest
1 cinnamon stick

½ tsp lemon juice
2 tsp vanilla
½ cup (120 ml) dark rum

Cake:
• Preheat the oven to 375°F (191°C).
• Butter an 9x13-inch (23x33-cm) baking dish and set aside.
• Sift the flour, salt, and baking powder into a large bowl.
• In a separate bowl, beat the egg whites and sugar until the mixture forms firm peaks. Add the yolks 1 by 1 until the egg whites and yolks are totally mixed, then add the vanilla. Add the flour mixture and mix well. Pour mixture into the prepared baking dish and bake for about 30—40 mins.
• Let the cake cool completely.

Syrup:
• In a saucepan combine the water and the sugar until the sugar melts. Add the lemon peel, the cinnamon stick and the lemon juice and let cook for 5 more minutes. Add the vanilla and cook for another minute. Let the mixture cool completely. Add the rum.
• Pour the syrup over the cake and let it soak in. Cut and serve.

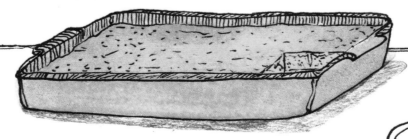

TORTICAS de MORÓN

Sugar Cookies with Lime Zest

Makes 20–24 cookies

These little sugar cookies hail from the city of Morón, located in the Ciego de Ávila province in central Cuba. They couldn't be easier to make, and go great with café cubano or even ice cream. Alternatively, try adding a bit of Grapefruit Marmalade (page 137) in the center of each before you bake them to make a thumbprint-style citrus cookie.

1 cup (184 g) shortening
1 cup (200 g) sugar
3 cups (360 g) all-purpose flour
1½ tsp lime zest

Preheat oven to 350°F (177°C). Beat together shortening and sugar until well blended. Slowly add flour to the mixture to make a smooth dough, then sprinkle in the lime zest and mix well.

Roll the dough out on a floured surface and cut out rounds with a 2-inch (5-cm) cookie cutter. Bake on a nonstick baking sheet for 20–25 mins. Cool on a wire rack.

BUÑUELOS

Sweet Fritters

Lots of countries make buñuelos, and shapes and recipes vary.
Mexican buñuelos are flat disks, while Spain makes spheres.
Cuban buñuelos are traditionally shaped in a figure 8
and made from a dough that always incorporates a couple of types
of viandas (root vegetables). They are often prepared
for Nochebuena (Christmas Eve).

MAKES 12–14

The Dough:

1 lb (450 g) yuca, peeled and cut into 2-inch (5-cm) pieces
1 lb (450 g) malanga, peeled and cut into 2-inch (5-cm) pieces
½ lb (230 g) boniato (sweet potato), peeled and cut into 2-inch (5-cm) pieces
1 Tbsp salt
3 eggs
3–4 cups (360–480 g) flour
Vegetable oil, for frying (I save my oil and use it over and over.)

The Syrup:

2 cups (475 ml) water
1 cup (200 g) sugar
1 whole star anise
1 cinnamon stick
2-inch (5-cm) strip lime zest
Juice from ½ lime

To make the dough, combine yuca, malanga, and boniato in a pot and cover with water. Cover pot, bring to a boil, and cook until soft. (Alternatively, cook in a pressure cooker with 1–2 inches (2.5–5 cm) water for 6–8 mins.)

While the vegetables cook, make the syrup by combining all ingredients except the lime juice. Bring to a boil, then reduce heat to low and simmer, stirring occasionally, until syrup has thickened, 20–25 mins. Remove from the heat and discard the lime zest. Stir in the lime juice and set aside.

Drain the vegetables. Remove any woody parts in the center of the yuca, and lay all vegetables on a kitchen towel to dry.

Working in batches, blend the warm vegetables in a food processor with the salt until smooth. On a floured surface, shape the vegetable mixture into a mound. Make a well in the center and add the eggs. Gently mix in the eggs with your hands, while gradually adding the flour to the dough. Knead the dough until it is smooth, but not sticky.

Divide the dough into 12–14 pieces, and roll each one with your hands into a long rope (about 14 inches/36 cm). Form each into a figure 8, connecting the ends.

Heat 2 inches (5 cm) of vegetable oil in a deep pan or Dutch oven over medium-high until it registers 375°F (191°C) on a deep-fry thermometer. Working in batches so as not to overcrowd the pan, fry buñuelos until golden brown, about 3 mins. Drain well on paper towels.

Drizzle the buñuelos with the syrup and enjoy!

Pastel de Guayaba

Makes 1 (9-inch/23-cm) Guava Pie

In Cuba, gas ovens are simple affairs, often lacking a pilot light or any sort of a controlled temperature. Carol Perez Bengochea, with whom I baked often in central Havana, smells, opens the oven door, looks, and touches the dessert to determine when it's done—using her senses all the while. This is a dessert prepared in a pinch. It's simple to make, quick, and calls for only a bar of guava paste (available at Latin markets) as filling.

2½ cups (300 g) unbleached all-purpose flour
2 Tbsp sugar
½ tsp salt
2 cups (450 g) cold unsalted butter or 1½ cups (350 ml) vegetable oil
(which is easier to find in Cuba than butter)
6 Tbsp cold water
1 (14-oz/400-g) bar pasta de guayaba (guava paste)

1. Sift the flour, sugar, and salt into a large bowl. Using a knife, cut the butter into the flour mixture and combine until the mixture resembles coarse commeal with pea-size lumps of butter. This can also be done with a stand mixer fitted with the whisk blade. Add the water and mix with a fork just until the dough pulls together.

2. Cut the dough in half and shape into discs. Dust the top of 1 disc with a little flour and roll out on a floured counter into a 12-inch (30-cm) diameter, about ½-inch (13 mm) thick circle, flipping halfway through. Repeat with the 2nd disc, then cover both with plastic wrap and chill in the fridge for about 30 mins.

3. Preheat oven to 420°F (216°C). Lay 1 piece of dough in a pie plate; remove the excess dough around edges. Cut the bar of guava paste into ¼-inch (6-mm) pieces and lay them in the pie.

4. Top the pie with the 2nd piece of dough and press down around the edges to seal. Use a fork to create a pattern along the edge and to poke a few ventilation holes in the top.

5. Bake until golden, 20—30 mins. Let cool completely before serving.

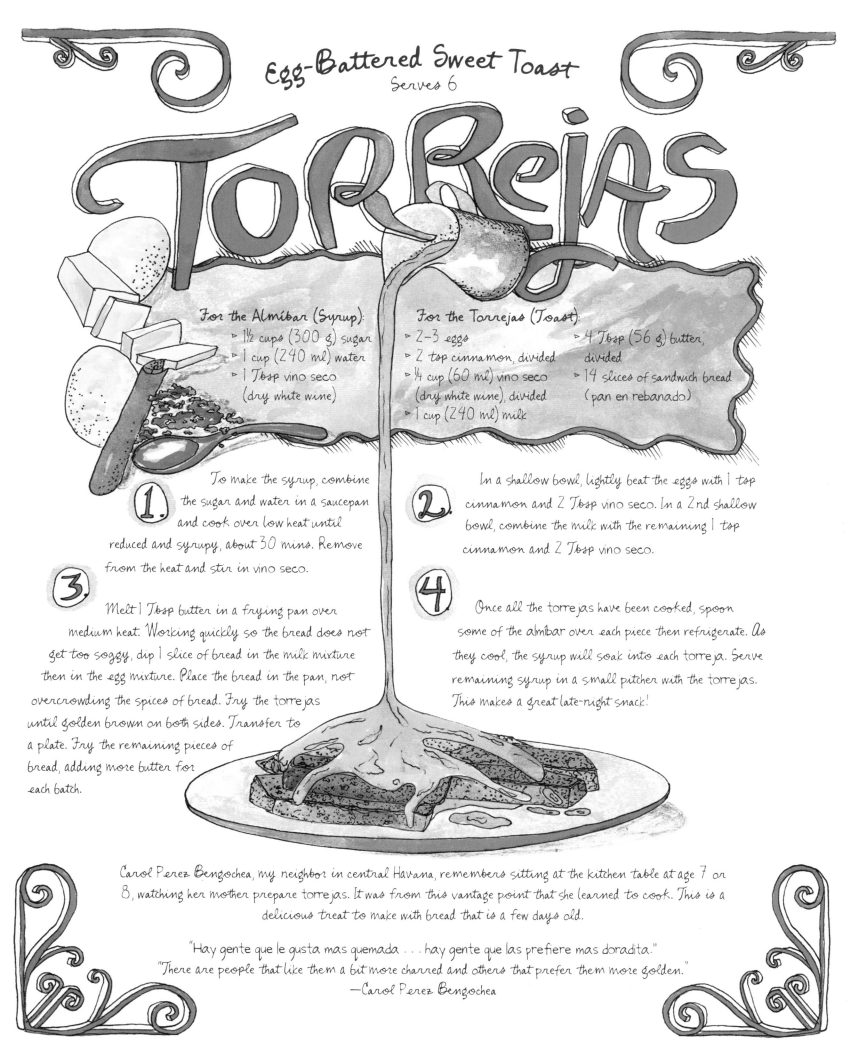

Torrejas

Egg-Battered Sweet Toast
Serves 6

For the Almíbar (Syrup):
- 1½ cups (300 g) sugar
- 1 cup (240 ml) water
- 1 Tbsp vino seco (dry white wine)

For the Torrejas (Toast):
- 2–3 eggs
- 2 tsp cinnamon, divided
- ¼ cup (60 ml) vino seco (dry white wine), divided
- 1 cup (240 ml) milk
- 4 Tbsp (56 g) butter, divided
- 14 slices of sandwich bread (pan en rebanado)

1. To make the syrup, combine the sugar and water in a saucepan and cook over low heat until reduced and syrupy, about 30 mins. Remove from the heat and stir in vino seco.

2. In a shallow bowl, lightly beat the eggs with 1 tsp cinnamon and 2 Tbsp vino seco. In a 2nd shallow bowl, combine the milk with the remaining 1 tsp cinnamon and 2 Tbsp vino seco.

3. Melt 1 Tbsp butter in a frying pan over medium heat. Working quickly so the bread does not get too soggy, dip 1 slice of bread in the milk mixture then in the egg mixture. Place the bread in the pan, not overcrowding the spices of bread. Fry the torrejas until golden brown on both sides. Transfer to a plate. Fry the remaining pieces of bread, adding more butter for each batch.

4. Once all the torrejas have been cooked, spoon some of the almíbar over each piece then refrigerate. As they cool, the syrup will soak into each torreja. Serve remaining syrup in a small pitcher with the torrejas. This makes a great late-night snack!

Carol Perez Bengochea, my neighbor in central Havana, remembers sitting at the kitchen table at age 7 or 8, watching her mother prepare torrejas. It was from this vantage point that she learned to cook. This is a delicious treat to make with bread that is a few days old.

"Hay gente que le gusta mas quemada . . . hay gente que las prefiere mas doradita."
"There are people that like them a bit more charred and others that prefer them more golden."
—Carol Perez Bengochea

Natilla

Serves 6

CUSTARD

Two Variations: Lemon Cream and Chocolate
Natilla is a rich and creamy egg-based custard that is great because it can be made completely ahead of a meal. The classic is a plain sweet milk flavor with a touch of lemon, but my favorite is chocolate. I will never forget Chef Antonio Solo's chocolate natilla served in a halved cacao pod, showcasing the finest chocolate from Baracoa.

- 4 cups (950 ml) whole milk
- 2-inch (5-cm) strip of lemon zest
  OR ½ cup (40 g) powdered baking chocolate
- 1 cinnamon stick
- ¼ teaspoon salt

- 1¼ cups (250 g) sugar
- 8 large egg yolks
- ¼ cup (28-g) cornstarch, dissolved in ¼ cup (60 ml) water
- 1 tsp pure vanilla extract
- Ground cinnamon, for garnish

1. In a saucepan heat milk, lemon zest (optional), cinnamon stick, and salt over medium heat and bring to a simmer, then remove from heat. In a large bowl using an electric mixer, on medium speed stir the sugar and egg yolks into a light yellow paste. Slowly add the cornstarch and baking chocolate (optional), and mixing constantly at low speed, integrate 2 cups (475 ml) of the hot milk.

2. Put the saucepan back over low heat, and combine the egg-and-milk mixture with the warm milk in the saucepan. Stir the mixture constantly with a whisk for 15–20 mins until the natilla is very thick. When texture is achieved, stir in the vanilla and discard the cinnamon stick and lemon zest.

3. Transfer the custard to serving bowls (or cacao pods if you have them). Cover with plastic wrap and refrigerate until chilled (2–3 hrs). Before serving, sprinkle the top with ground cinnamon as garnish.

Harina Dulce
DE MAÍZ

Sweet Cornmeal Pudding • Serves 6

This is a dessert very familiar to guajiros (a term for country folk in Cuba), who utilize the ground corn abundant in the countryside to make a sweet polenta pudding. When fresh milk isn't available, Cubans often substitute powdered milk, sweetened condensed milk, or just water to make this basic dessert. Adjust sugar and salt to taste when using these alternate ingredients.

8 cups (940 ml) water
1 tsp salt
1 cinnamon stick
1-inch (2.5 cm) strip lemon zest
2 cups (280 g) fine cornmeal
1½ cups (350 ml) whole milk
1 cup (200 g) sugar
1 tsp vanilla

Bring the water to a boil in a saucepan, then add salt, cinnamon, and lemon zest. While whisking, slowly add the cornmeal and keep whisking as the mixture thickens. Add the milk, sugar, and vanilla. Continue to gently cook over very low heat for about 30 mins, stirring occasionally, until mixture is creamy.

Drizzle a little honey and a sprinkle of ground cinnamon over each portion to serve.

DULCE de Toronja

Candied Grapefruit Rind • Makes about 8 cups (600 g)

This is a pretty candy to make around the holidays and share with family and friends. It's a big recipe, but any leftover can be made into marmalade.

- 5 grapefruits
- 6 cups (1.2 kg) white sugar
- 2 cups (426 g) light brown sugar
- 4 cups (950 ml) water
- 1 Tbsp fresh lime juice
- 1 cinnamon stick

Carefully peel grapefruits, removing and discarding the thin, outer pink-yellow zest*. With the bald-looking whole grapefruits, cut each in half, score around the inner edge of the white pith with a knife, and peel out the fruit; set aside for another use**. Cut the pith halves into eighths and place in a bowl. Add water to cover and soak overnight with a plate that fits inside the bowl to keep grapefruit immersed in water.

The next morning, drain and add enough fresh water to a pot to cover the grapefruit. Boil the pith of the grapefruit, covered, for 15 mins. Drain, then add enough fresh water to cover the rind and boil it again. Repeat this process at least 3 times, which reduces the rind's bitterness. By the end, the grapefruit rind will appear somewhat translucent and light pink in color. Drain well, and transfer the rinds to paper towels to cool,

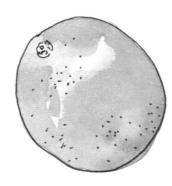

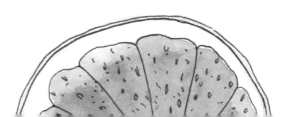

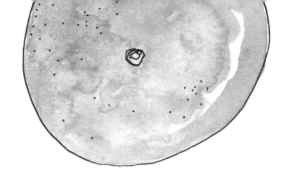

then squeeze the moisture from each piece with your hands.

Combine the white and brown sugars, 4 cups (950 ml) water, the lime juice, and the cinnamon stick. Cook over medium heat until the sugar melts and mixture thickens, about 5 mins. Add the grapefruit and cook at very low heat until the syrup is thick but not caramelized, about 2 hrs. Remove from the heat and take candied grapefruit out of syrup, placing on a cookie sheet to cool.

Will keep up to 1 week in sealed container or 1 month refrigerated.

Use zest as a cleaning agent: Boil ½ cup (48 g) grapefruit zest in 4 cups (950 ml) vinegar for 10 min. Let cool. Store in a spray bottle and use as a surface cleaner.
**If not eating out of hand, use the leftover fruit to make fresh juice: Combine the fruit with ½ cup (120 ml) water in a blender and blend. Strain and discard pulp before drinking.

Mermelada de Toronja (Grapefruit Marmalade):
Follow the above instructions. Strain the candied rind pieces from the syrup and place in a food processor or blender and process. Store in sterilized containers in the fridge. The syrup can be diluted and used in the Panatela recipe (see page 128).

Serve with a fresh, mild cheese on toast or use as a filling for Pastelitos (page 111) or Empanadas (page 116).

137

CÓCTELES

Cocktails

AROMATICO

Spiced

So called because of the addition of citrus fruits and fragrant herbs, such as rosemary or cloves, that complement the spirit's butterscotch tones. Spiced rums are usually sipped over ice or topped with ginger beer.

BLANCO

White

Distilled for a short period of time and filtered with charcoal to make it clear, this is the mildest and most delicate rum and complements fruity drinks.

DORADO

Gold

Aged in oak barrels, this rum is ideal in robust, sweet cocktails, like the Cuba Libre.

NEGRO

Black or Dark

This dark rum is aged in charred oak barrels for longer than the gold rum varieties.

The Types of Rum

Ron en la Isla
Rum on the Island

The sugar industry increased steadily throughout the 16th century on the island of Cuba. At the time, molasses, the byproduct of sugar production, was considered waste that was fed to livestock and rarely consumed by people. However, the sugar farmers had more of this sticky substance than they knew what to do with. It wasn't until the 1600s that people discovered they could mix molasses with some of the liquid from the sugarcane juice during its initial boiling to make an alcoholic spirit. This mixture was left to ferment and then distilled—and a predecessor of rum was born. They soon knew they were onto something, and rum production continued to evolve.

By 1860, there were more than 1,000 distilleries in Cuba, including one owned by Spanish entrepreneur Don Facundo Bacardí in partnership with French distiller and confectioner José León Bouteiller. The men were among those who experimented widely and implemented methods to create a more palatable, lighter-bodied alcohol. The use of charcoal filtration gave way to the first light-colored rum. Copper stills, storage in oak barrels, and the use of specific strains of yeast to accelerate the fermentation process further improved the flavor and depth of the rum. Today, rum is produced all over the world, but everyone knows the best rum comes from Cuba.

Although most locals imbibe their rum simply on the rocks (usually crushed ice), many cocktail recipes abound—developed for the tourist trade. Most of these recipes are inspired by the island itself, including the *Cuba Libre* and the *Cubita*. In the US, rum cocktails gained popularity during World War II, when grain rations restricted whiskey and beer production. After the war and into the 1950s, the little island 90 miles off the coast of Florida became America's playground, and rum drinks were all the rage.

MOJITO

Serves 1

This iconic drink never fails to evoke the enchantment and beauty of Cuba. Iterations of the mojito have been consumed by pirates, the Spanish crown, the Mafia, and even Michelle Obama. It has a deep-rooted history and is said to have been invented by slaves who made it with *aguardiente* (literally "fire water," a harsh-tasting spirit). Eventually this was replaced by the smoother, more delicate white rum in the 1900s.

- 3 sprigs spearmint*
  with stems (about 10 leaves)
- 1½ tsp superfine sugar
- 1 oz (30 ml) fresh lime juice
- Crushed ice
- 2½ oz (75 ml) white rum
- Club soda
- 2 dashes Angostura bitters
- Slice of lime

Rub the mint leaves around the rim of a Collins glass. Combine 2 mint sprigs, sugar, and lime juice in the glass. Stir with a teaspoon to dissolve the sugar, then lightly pound the mint to muddle it. Add enough crushed ice to fill ¾ of the glass, then add the rum. Top off with club soda. Garnish with bitters, lime juice, and remaining sprig of mint.

Variations:

Mojito de Miel: In the countryside of Cuba, I encountered more honey on the menu and at the market than in Havana. I suppose I was closer to the producers. It was in the town of Matanzas that I tried a *Mojito de Miel*. Prepare the basic mojito, but replace the sugar with honey.

Mojito Imperial: Replace the mojito's club soda with sparkling wine.

*Spearmint is known as *yerba buena*, which is the main variety of mint in Cuba.

DAIQUIRI

Serves 1

The daiquiri was named for a beach in Santiago de Cuba, but Ernest Hemingway made it famous. The American writer lived near Havana in the 1940s and 1950s and famously used Cuba as a backdrop for some of his writings and books, including *The Old Man and the Sea*. Hemingway frequented a bar near Havana, Floridita, known for serving the best daiquiris on the island. A small plaque hanging in the bar displays Hemingway's signed quote: "My mojito in La Bodeguita (del Medio) My daiquiri in El Floridita."

- 2 oz (60 ml) white rum
- 1 tsp caster sugar
- ¾ oz (20 ml) fresh lime juice
- 1 tsp maraschino liqueur
- Ice
- Lime slice

Combine the rum, sugar, lime juice, liqueur, and ice in a shaker. Shake well, then strain into a chilled tulip or martini glass. Garnish with a slice of lime.

Frozen Daiquiri: Put all ingredients in a blender along with ice and blend well.

Hemingway Daiquiri: My favorite version adds 2 oz (60 ml) fresh grapefruit juice to the classic daiquiri recipe.

141

Coca-Cola arrived in Cuba at the turn of the 20th century. The creation of the Cuba Libre coincided with Cuba declaring its independence from Spain.

CUBA Libre

Serves 1

▷ ½ lime
▷ Ice cubes
▷ 2 oz (60 ml) white rum
▷ Coca-Cola

Squeeze the lime juice into a Collins glass and drop the squeezed lime shells into the glass. Add 3 large ice cubes and pour in the rum. Top off with cold Coca-Cola. Stir to combine.

142   Variation: Try a Cubata! This is a Cuba Libre made with añejo (aged) dark rum in place of white rum.

PIÑA Colada

Makes 1 drink

In Havana, people often make their piña coladas with powdered milk, which has long been the most accessible milk around. On the eastern part of the island, people often replace cow's milk with fresh coconut milk to lend a creamy richness to the drink.

- 1 cup (225 g) chopped pineapple
- 1 cup (240 ml) water
- ¼ cup (35 g) powdered milk
- 2 Tbsp sugar
- 2 oz (60 ml) light rum
- 1 cup (215 g) crushed ice

Combine the pineapple and water in a blender and blend until smooth. Pour the mixture through a fine-mesh sieve. Return the pineapple juice to the blender. Add the powdered milk, sugar, rum, and crushed ice and blend until smooth. Serve with a wedge of pineapple on the rim of a glass.

GUANTANAMERA

Perhaps Cuba's most loved song, "Guantanamera" was written by Julián Orbón who adapted it from a poem by José Martí. Famous for his dedication to the goal of Cuba's freedom from Spain, Martí's heartfelt and powerful writings have inspired those fighting for independence all over Latin America. The song is written from the perspective of a common man in love with a woman from Guantánamo who eventually leaves him. Though sad, the song has a very positive side in its patriotic symbolism and uplifting melody.

La Canción:

Yo soy un hombre sincero
De donde crece la palma
Y antes de morirme quiero
Echar mis versos del alma

I am a truthful man
From where the palm tree grows
And before dying I want
To let out the verses of my soul

Guantanamera,
guajira Guantanamera

Mi verso es de un verde claro
Y de un carmín encendido
Mi verso es un ciervo herido
Que busca en el monte amparo

My verse is light green
And it is flaming red
My verse is a wounded stag
Who seeks refuge on the mountain

Guantanamera,
guajira Guantanamera

Cultivo una rosa blanca
En julio como en enero
Para el amigo sincero
Que me da su mano franca

I grow a white rose
In July just as in January
For the honest friend
Who gives me his open hand

Guantanamera,
guajira Guantanamera

Con los pobres de la tierra
Quiero yo mi suerte echar
El arroyo de la sierra
Me complace más que el mar

With the poor people of the earth
I want to cast my lot
The brook of the mountains
Gives me more pleasure than the sea

Guantanamera,
guajira Guantanamera

Leche de COCO

HUSK

CORE

SHELL

MEAT

WATER

Fresh coconut milk tastes so much better than canned—the flavor is rich, bright, and well worth the effort. Making a batch doesn't take too long, especially if you use a food processor! I learned how in Baracoa, on the east end of the island, the region known for its coconut production and dishes showcasing coconut milk.

- 1 brown, mature coconut (not the green kind with the shell still on)
  When selecting a coconut, make sure you can hear the
  coconut water inside and that the "eyes" are firm, not at all soft.

1. Use a screwdriver to make holes through the eyes of the coconut and drain out the water inside. Reserve.

2. In a dry pan, heat the whole coconut over medium-high heat, rotating every minute until it cracks open, about 10 mins. Seal the coconut in a bag and hit it with a hammer. Pry the meat carefully out of each piece of the shell. Using a vegetable peeler, peel off any remaining bits. The meat should be bright white.

3. Measure the coconut water and add enough hot tap water to measure 2 cups (475 ml) total; pour into a food processor along with the coconut meat. Process until the mixture is frothy and thick, 4–6 mins. The hot water helps extract as much of the flavor as possible. (Alternately, finely shred the coconut and combine with the liquids to soak for 10 mins.)

4. Strain the mixture through a fine-mesh sieve lined with cheesecloth, pressing on it to extract as much of the coconut milk as possible. You will be left with dry shredded coconut, which can be reserved for another use. Coconut milk will keep for up to 3 days in the fridge.

CUBANITO

Makes 1 drink

A tangy, tomato-based cocktail with the Cuban spirit of choice—rum!—a close relation to a Bloody Mary.

- Ice
- 2 tsp fresh lime juice
- 1½ oz (43 ml) white rum
- 3 oz (85 ml) tomato juice
- 1 tsp Worcestershire sauce
- Drops of your favorite cayenne hot sauce
- Pinch of salt
- Garnish: slice of lime

Fill a tumbler halfway with ice. Pour in lime juice, rum, and tomato juice. Add Worcestershire, hot sauce, and salt and stir well to combine. Garnish with lime.

Canchánchara

Honey Rum Cocktail • Serves 1

This drink is famous in the town of Trinidad, one of Cuba's most well-preserved cities, which is nestled in the beautiful Valle de los Ingenios and dates back to the 1500s. Hot and tired from a morning horseback ride, we stopped at a little paladar, where I enjoyed my first canchánchara, served in the traditional small, round terra-cotta cups with aguardiente and wild honey.

▷ Juice of 1 lime

▷ 2 Tbsp honey

▷ 1½ oz (43 ml) aguardiente or your favorite rum

▷ Crushed ice

Combine the lime juice, honey, and aguardiente in a cocktail shaker and stir until the honey dissolves. Add crushed ice and shake well. Strain into a glass or serve on the rocks.

CREMA de Vie

Cuban Eggnog • Serves 6—8

Traditionally prepared for the holidays, this drink—the "cream of life"—is super-rich, and a little goes a long way. It's a sipping dessert.

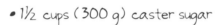

- 1½ cups (300 g) caster sugar
- 1½ cups (350 ml) water
- 1 cinnamon stick
- 1 (14-oz/400-g) can evaporated milk
- 1 (14-oz/400-g) can sweetened condensed milk
- 3 egg yolks
- 1 tsp vanilla
- 2 cups (475 ml) rum or brandy

Make a simple syrup by combining the sugar, water, and cinnamon stick in a saucepan and simmering over low heat until the sugar is dissolved, about 10 mins.

In a blender, combine the milks, yolks, and vanilla and blend until well combined. Transfer to a glass container. Stir in the rum and the simple syrup, including the cinnamon stick. Refrigerate until ready to serve. Serve in small cups.

Sangria

el estilo Cubano

Cuban-Style Sangria

Makes approximately 1½ gallons (5.5 L)

1 (750ml) bottle, full-bodied, red wine
8 oz (240ml) orange juice
8 oz (240ml) rum
Juice of 1 lime

2 oranges, peeled and chopped
1 cup (175 g) halved grapes
2 cups (450 ml) pineapple, chopped
32 oz (950 ml) club soda

Combine wine, orange juice, rum, lime juice, and fruit. Let sit for at least 2 hours in a large bowl.

Add club soda and serve in a punch bowl or large pitcher with ice.

Glossary

Achiote
Annato. A small red seed from a pod plant, used primarily to color food. Very mild flavor, can be purchased ground or whole, and may be combined with oil. Often referred to as "bija."

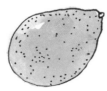

Aguacate/Avocado
Cuban avocados, like those grown in Florida, are large and bright green on the outside. If not using the whole avocado, save the side with the seed in a sealed container in the refrigerator, so that it does not oxidize.

Aguardiente
An unrefined alcohol made of sugarcane.

Ají
The common term for spicy pepper.

Ají Ancho
Also known as the cubanelle or mild Italian frying pepper.

Ají Cachucha
Similar in appearance to a habanero, but not spicy. Also referred to as ají dulce, it is fruity in flavor. Starts out green then matures to red and orange on the vine.

Ají Chay
Looks like a small jalapeño, but lends an acidic, fruity flavor. Mild in spice.

Ají Guaguao
Also known as ají picante, this very spicy, small red pepper is similar to a Thai chile and is one of the only spicy peppers cultivated in Cuba.

Aliño
A salad dressing made with lime or vinegar.

Almíbar
A simple syrup used in many Cuban desserts, including soaked cakes and stewed fruit.

Bijól
A brand name blend of achiote, corn flour, and food coloring created by Rafael Martínez in 1922 to lend color to a dish. It is often used as a substitute for saffron. I recommend just using achiote/bija (annatto).

Boniato
Sweet potato native to Africa.

Buñuelo
A doughnutlike fritter that is typically served with an almíbar, a light sugar syrup.

Casabe/Yuca Flatbread
Bread that the native Ciboney Indians made from the yuca root.

Chayote
A pear-shaped summer squash with pale green skin and a large seed. Prepare as you would a squash.

Chícharos
Split peas.

Chorizo • Spicy Spanish Sausage
This paprika-rich, fresh pork sausage is used in a variety of Cuban dishes, especially in stews of Spanish origin.

Coco Seco/Dry Coconut
A ripened dark brown coconut that still has some liquid inside. Shake each coconut before buying it to be sure that it contains liquid; if it doesn't, it is likely to be spoiled.

Culantro
Not to be confused with cilantro, this flavorful herb is used throughout the Caribbean. Its flavor is similar to cilantro, but much stronger.

Enchilado
A fresh tomato and bell pepper sauce used often with seafood.

Falda/Flank Steak
An economical cut of beef that shreds well after long cooking. Used in *ropa vieja* and *vaca frita*.

Fruta Bomba
Another term for papaya.

Guarapo/Sugarcane Juice
Often made by passing the sugarcane stalk through a hand-cranked press to extract the juice. Sold fresh from street vendors and served with ice.

Harina de Maíz/Cornmeal
Finely ground cornmeal that is cooked to make polenta or porridge. Often served like rice, under a stewed main dish.

Yerba Buena/Mint
Similar to spearmint and the preferred type of mint to make a mojito. The leaves have a milder flavor than peppermint, and some types have purple stems.

Jamón de Cocinar/Cooking Ham
The ham used for cooking in Cuba is cured raw ham, similar to *jamón serrano* from Spain. It is usually sold as a slab or in chunks.

Limón/Lime
Not to be mistaken for lemons, which are rarely used. Most limes are what North Americans call Persian limes. *Limones criollos* are also used, these small, round limes are known as Key limes in the US.

Mamey Sapote
A rich, sweet, creamy tree fruit whose pink flesh resembles that of an avocado in texture.

Mojo
A blended sauce of garlic, oil, citrus, and salt. Mojo can be used as a marinade or served with vegetables.

Moros y Cristianos
The Spanish phrase for the mixture of black beans and white rice, which means "Moors and Christians."

Ñame
African white yam.

Naranja Agria
Sour orange.

Orégano de la Tierra/Orégano Cubano
A highly aromatic, succulent herb, it has a large leaf with serrated edges. Technically part of the mint family.

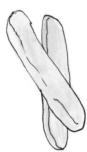

Pan Cubano
Cuban bread. Similar to a French baguette but not nearly as crusty, with a very soft interior. I never saw anyone making bread at home in Cuba; most people buy it at their local panadería.

Picadillo
A savory dish made of ground beef and sofrito. Cooks often add raisins, olives, almonds, capers, and cubed potatoes. Can be used as a filling for tostones, empanadas, and pastelitos.

Plancha
Sandwich press. Used for making any toasted sandwiches; an essential tool in cafeterías.

Plátanos
Plantains.

Quimbombó
Okra. These fresh green pods native to Africa are used in a several Afro-Cuban dishes.

Sofrito
A combination of sautéed vegetables, herbs, and spices. Includes the trinity of chopped peppers, onions, and garlic—the flavor base of most Cuban dishes.

Tasajo
A dried, salt-cured beef that needs to be soaked in water before using.

Tostones
Twice-fried green plantain disks, smashed using a tostonera—2 wooden planks hinged together.

Viandas
Starchy vegetables such as malanga, boniato, yuca, calabaza, and plantains.

Vino Seco
A mildly salty, dry white cooking wine. Can substitute a dry white wine.

Yuca
Cassava, a starchy browned-skinned tuber.

Acknowledgments

Many thanks to the following people for their generosity, expertise, and time lent to this project. To the incredible people who shared their recipes and *secretos de la cocina*, and spent their afternoons, sometimes days, cooking with me. To those who assisted me on the journey to and around Cuba. To Christopher Graham and the many loved ones who assisted in the test kitchen phase, and provided critical feedback when I needed it most. To my mom, Paulina Kriebel, for helping with the whole project, and being my sounding board for so many of the drawings and recipes—always just a phone call away. To Kate Winslow for her dedication to the project from start to finish, and for such solid guidance when looking at the project from a bird's-eye view. To Tony Rossodivito and fellow scholars of Cuban history, anthropology, and economics for teaching me so much about the dynamic and distinct history and culture of Cuba. To my arts community in Washington, DC, who documented the process and offered daily support. To Janet and Buz Teacher for believing in me and conceiving the the idea for this book.

Special Thanks

Alberto Gámez Ronda

Yoeluis Binimelias

Antonio Solo

Invalis Guilbeaux Rodríguez

Carol Perez Bengochea

Eloisa Hernández Janeiro

Ana Maria and Jorge Ventosa

Pedro and Martica Duperey

Idaliana Legrá Puig

María Magdalena Domínguez Cubero

Isabel González Herrera

Lázaro Chirino Padrón

Maraldo Garcia Calderón

Gladys and Samy

Sapayo

Dr. Manuel Yepe

Hanna Garth

Catherine Murphy

Buz and Janet Teacher

Maria Gonzalez

Emelio Companioni

Ken Newbaker

Thom O'Hearn

Erin McCluskey

Charlotte Wells

Asori Soto

Doug Dyer

John Connell-Maribona

Jim Ryerson

Robin Groth

Etta Ettlinger and Wells Todd

Michael Todd

Greg Kriebel

Dustin Kriebel

Marco Vinicio Fiallo

Russ Brooks

Charlene Murdock and Richard White

Jewish Food Experience

Bates House Family

The Arts Walk Community

Adelante Mujeres

Index

photo Victoria Milko

About the Author

Marcella Kriebel is an artist and author based in Washington, DC, best known for her vibrant watercolors and dynamic line drawings celebrating food. Her sketchbooks, filled with hand-drawn recipes from her travels in Latin America, became the backbone for her first cookbook, *Mi Comida Latina*. *Comida Cubana* is the second book offered in Marcella's unique style, featuring detailed watercolor illustrations and dynamic layouts, of both classic dishes and inspiring new combinations from the entire island. In addition to cookbooks, Marcella is the creator of the collection *Illustrated Feast*, an extensive, open-edition series of watercolor prints available at select retailers, seasonal markets, online, and at her studio on the Arts Walk, Brookland in Washington, DC. Her work has been featured in the blog *Design Sponge*, *The Washington Post*, and National Public Radio.

IDEAS del MENÚ
(Menu Ideas)

Pascua / EASTER

Garapiña (Fermented Pineapple Juice) page 103
Arroz con Mariscos (Rice with Seafood) page 46
Pargo al Homo (Baked Snapper) page 74
Crema de Berro (Cream of Watercress) page 91
Ensalada de Calabaza (Squash Salad) page 86
Pastelitos con Mermelada (Jam Pastries) page 116

Dia de la Mama Desayuno-Almuerzo
MOTHER'S DAY BRUNCH

Café Cubano (Cuban Coffee) page 108
Cubanitos (Cuban Bloody Mary) page 146
Tostones Rellenos (Stuffed Plantain Cups) page 83
Pollo Asado Relleno de Moros (Roast Chicken Stuffed with Rice & Beans) page 20
Ensalada de Piña y Aguacate (Pineapple & Avocado Salad) page 99
Flan de Calabaza (Squash Flan) page 123

Fiesta de Graduación
GRADUATION PARTY

Canchánchara (Honey Rum Cocktail) page 147
Pernil Asado (Roast Pork) page 24
Congrí (Black Beans & Rice) page 55
Yuca con Mojo (Yuca with Citrus Dressing) page 87
La Ensalada Mixta (Mixed Salad) page 95
Plátanos Fritos (Fried Sweet Plantains) page 80

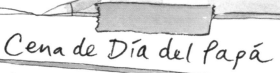

Cena de Día del Papá
FATHERS DAY DINNER

Mojito (Rum & Mint Cocktail) page 140
Jaibas Rellenas (Stuffed Blue Crab Shells) page 67
Quimbombó con Plátano (Okra with Plantains) page 85
Ropa Vieja (Stewed Shredded Beef) page 34
Congrí (Rice & Beans) page 55
Dulce de Fruta Bomba (Candied Papaya) page 124